Bitcoin: The NEW GOLD

The Asset of Freedom and Security

in a World of Uncertainty

GIANNIS ANDREOU

Gems of Thought

"I'm a big believer in Bitcoin—it's bigger than any government. I do believe it is an alternative source for wealth holding. If you're in a country where you're fearful of your future, your government, or its currency devaluation due to deficits, Bitcoin is a great potential long-term store of value. It's like digital gold."

- Larry Fink, CEO of BlackRock

"Bitcoin is no different than what gold has represented for thousands of years. It is an asset class that protects you."

- Larry Fink, CEO of BlackRock

"Our base case for Bitcoin is $600,000. In a bull case, $1.5 million by 2030."

- Cathie Wood, CEO of ARK Invest

"Allocating up to 2% of your portfolio to Bitcoin is reasonable."

- Ray Dalio, Founder of Bridgewater Associates

"The value of Bitcoin can never be negative. It's no coincidence that cryptocurrencies, which have some semblance of control and correct math, are doing well."

- Alan Greenspan, Former Chair of the Federal Reserve

"Managing $108 billion in assets, VanEck forecasts that the price of Bitcoin could reach $2.9 million by the year 2050."

- VanEck Investment Firm

"Leading a $13.2 billion firm, Cantor Fitzgerald predicts that major banks and traditional financial institutions will dive headfirst into Bitcoin if regulatory conditions improve."

- Cantor Fitzgerald's CEO

"If elected president, I will make the United States the crypto capital of the planet."

- Donald Trump, President of the United States

"We're in the Bitcoin gold rush. It will last for 10 years."

- Michael Saylor, Executive Chairman of MicroStrategy

"Bitcoin is a technological tour de force."

- Bill Gates, Co-founder of Microsoft

"It's money 2.0, a huge, huge, huge deal."

- Chamath Palihapitiya, Founder of Social Capital

"Bitcoin is a remarkable cryptographic achievement, and the ability to create something that is not duplicable in the digital world has enormous value."

- Eric Schmidt, Former CEO of Google

"I do think Bitcoin is the first [encrypted money] that has the potential to do something like change the world."

- Peter Thiel, Co-founder of PayPal

"The world ultimately will have a single currency; the internet will have a single currency. I personally believe that it will be Bitcoin."

- Jack Dorsey, CEO of Twitter and Square

"Bitcoin is a far better way to transfer value than pieces of paper."

- Elon Musk, CEO of Tesla and SpaceX

"I like Bitcoin even more now than I did then. I think we are in the first inning of Bitcoin, and it's got a long way to go."

- Paul Tudor Jones, Billionaire Hedge Fund Manager

"I'm a believer... I'm one of the few standing before you today from a large financial services company that has not given up on digital currencies."

- Abigail Johnson, CEO of Fidelity Investments

These perspectives underscore the diverse and growing recognition of Bitcoin's potential across various sectors.

On August 20, 2024, Bitcoin Magazine revealed that 60% of the world's top 25 hedge funds have disclosed their Bitcoin #Bitcoin BTC ETF holdings. Among them:

HEDGE FUND	QUANTITY OF BTC OWNED	ADDED ON 2nd QUARTER '24
Citadel Investment Group	812	41
Millennium Management	27,263	1,429
Mariner Investment Group	930	493
Balyasny Asset Management	6	6
Renaissance Technologies	286	152
Point72 Asset Management	1,089	
D.E. Shaw	132	
Verition Fund Management	93	
G.S. Asset Management	6,202	6,202
Schonfeld Strategic Advisors	6,734	
Bluecrest Capital Management	9	
Fortress Investment Group	1,181	428
Elliot Investment Management	1,092	924
Two Sigma Investments	458	428
Sculptor Capital Management	876	

Data source: theblockbeats.info

Disclaimer

The information provided in this book is for educational and informational purposes only and should not be considered investment or financial advice. I am not a licensed financial advisor. I have been personally involved in Bitcoin since 2012, including operating my own Bitcoin mining company, and have dedicated thousands of hours over a decade to researching the cryptocurrency space.

This book is intended to provide you with information to help you make informed investment decisions, but ultimately, the decision to invest and the amount to invest are entirely your own.

Investing in Bitcoin, like any other investment, carries inherent risks. Markets are influenced by various unpredictable factors, including geopolitical events, shifts in the global economy, and unforeseen circumstances. No matter how promising an investment may seem, risks remain an integral part of the process.

If you need additional guidance, please consult a qualified financial professional to understand your specific situation and risk tolerance better. Always remember: informed decisions are the cornerstone of successful investing.

It is up to you to agree or disagree with the views or ideas presented.

I may have financial interests in certain cryptocurrencies or companies discussed in this book. This book contains links and QR codes that are referral links.

GLOSSARY

At the end of this book there is a glossary with definitions of the terms you will encounter as you read it. I suggest that you find the terms in the glossary that you do not fully understand while reading the book, and read their definitions to get a better understanding of the text and data.

Acknowledgments

First and foremost, I want to extend my deepest gratitude to you, my audience. Your unwavering support, engagement, and curiosity about cryptocurrency inspire me daily. With your questions, comments, and shared enthusiasm, you have pushed me to dig deeper, learn more, and strive to provide the most valuable insights I can.

To my family and friends, thank you for standing by me through all the highs and lows of this journey. Your belief in me and your constant encouragement have been my anchor. Without your support, this book—and everything leading up to it—wouldn't have been possible.

This book is as much yours as it is mine, a testament to the shared journey we're all on in this revolutionary era of financial freedom. Here's to a future shaped by innovation, resilience, and the pursuit of knowledge.

Table of Contents

Introduction: The Fight for Financial Freedom

Imagine a world where your hard-earned money loses its value overnight due to inflation, where the financial system is rigged to favor the privileged few while the rest struggle to stay afloat. Now, imagine an alternative—a financial revolution built on transparency, fairness, and individual empowerment. That revolution is Bitcoin.

From its mysterious inception in 2009, Bitcoin has captured the imagination of technologists, economists, and visionaries. It emerged as a response to one of the greatest financial crises of our time, promising not just a new currency but a new way of thinking about money itself. Today, Bitcoin is no longer just an experiment; it's a global phenomenon reshaping the foundations of wealth, trust, and freedom.

Why This Book Matters Now

The world we live in today is more interconnected than ever, but it's also fraught with uncertainty. Governments print trillions of dollars in fiat currency, eroding the value of savings. Banks impose barriers to entry, leaving billions unbanked or underserved. Economic inequality continues to widen, fueling discontent and mistrust. Bitcoin offers a way out—a decentralized, borderless, and censorship-resistant form of money that empowers individuals to take control of their financial destiny.

This book isn't just about understanding Bitcoin; it's about understanding the moment we live in. It's about asking hard questions: What happens when trust in traditional institutions erodes? How can individuals protect themselves in a world of economic turbulence? And, most importantly, how can we leverage technology to create a fairer and more inclusive financial future?

The Heart of the Bitcoin Revolution

Bitcoin is more than a digital currency; it's a movement. At its core is the idea of decentralization—removing the need for intermediaries like banks and governments to control your money. It's a system that runs on trustless technology, where cryptographic proof replaces human corruption. Every transaction is verified on a public ledger, ensuring transparency while preserving privacy. Bitcoin isn't just money; it's freedom encoded in digital form.

For millions around the world, Bitcoin has already changed lives. In Venezuela, where hyperinflation renders the local currency worthless, Bitcoin has become a lifeline for families to store value and buy essentials. In Nigeria, it's fueling a tech-savvy generation of entrepreneurs who bypass traditional banking altogether. And for institutional investors on Wall Street, Bitcoin is emerging as the ultimate hedge against an unpredictable future.

But the story of Bitcoin is far from over. As we'll explore in this book, Bitcoin is evolving. Its adoption is accelerating, its use cases are expanding, and its impact on the global financial system is only just the beginning. From being dismissed as a speculative bubble to being embraced by billion-dollar corporations and governments, Bitcoin's journey is a testament to its resilience and transformative power.

What This Book Offers

This book is not a dry technical manual or a one-sided sales pitch for Bitcoin. It's an invitation to explore, question, and engage with one of the most disruptive innovations of our time. It's written for anyone who's curious—whether you're a complete beginner wondering what Bitcoin is all about or a seasoned investor seeking deeper insights.

Here's what you can expect:

- A journey through the origins of Bitcoin and the mysterious figure of Satoshi Nakamoto.
- An exploration of the revolutionary technology behind Bitcoin—blockchain, mining, and decentralization—in simple, accessible language.
- Insights into how Bitcoin is reshaping economies, empowering individuals, and challenging the status quo.
- Perspectives from key opinion leaders, from BlackRock's Larry Fink to Ark Invest's Cathie Wood, and why they believe Bitcoin is the future of finance.
- A balanced discussion of Bitcoin's risks, challenges, and potential to transform into a global reserve currency.
- Practical strategies for understanding, investing in, and thriving with Bitcoin.

Why This Story Resonates

What makes this book different? It's not just about Bitcoin; it's about what Bitcoin represents: the fight for greater financial freedom and economic sovereignty. It's about understanding why money matters, how it shapes our lives, and how we can regain control over our financial destiny. In a world where financial literacy is often reserved for the elite, Bitcoin is leveling the playing field, empowering anyone with internet access to participate in a global economy.

This is a story of innovation, courage, and the unrelenting pursuit of freedom. It's a story that will inspire you, challenge you, and maybe even change the way you think about money. By reading this book, you're not just learning about Bitcoin; you're gaining insights into the future of finance.

Part 1. The Genesis of Bitcoin

This part sets the historical foundation for the book, exploring how and why Bitcoin came into existence. It will captivate readers with the story of its creation, the mysterious figure of Satoshi Nakamoto, and the broader context of the 2008 financial crisis.

The Financial Crisis of 2008: The Catalyst for Bitcoin

In 2008, the world was thrust into a devastating economic collapse—a severe financial crisis that shattered trust in traditional financial systems and reshaped the global economy. The meltdown began in the United States but rapidly spread across the globe, leaving a wake of bankruptcies, job losses, and public disillusionment with banks, governments, and financial institutions.

The Roots of the Crisis

At the heart of the 2008 crisis was a toxic cocktail of greed, mismanagement, and systemic failure. For years, banks and financial institutions had engaged in irresponsible lending practices, offering subprime mortgages—loans to individuals with poor credit histories who were unlikely to repay them. These mortgages were bundled into complex financial instruments called mortgage-backed securities (MBS) and misrepresented as low-risk to investors worldwide.

Credit rating agencies played a pivotal role in exacerbating the problem by assigning high ratings to these risky securities, misleading investors into believing they were safe. Fuelled by a climate of deregulation, the housing market soared, and everyone—from Wall Street executives to average homeowners—felt like they were winning.

But this house of cards was built on shaky foundations. When housing prices began to decline in 2007, the entire system started to unravel. Homeowners defaulted on their loans in record numbers, and the value of mortgage-backed securities plummeted. Banks, many of which had leveraged themselves heavily to profit from this market, found themselves insolvent almost overnight.

The Collapse

By September 2008, the crisis reached a boiling point. Lehman Brothers, a 158-year-old investment bank, declared bankruptcy, triggering panic in financial markets worldwide. Major institutions like Bear Stearns, Merrill Lynch, and AIG teetered on the brink of collapse. Governments were forced to intervene, pumping billions of dollars into bailouts to prevent a total economic meltdown.

The crisis exposed the fragility of the financial system and the deep interconnectedness of global economies. What began as a housing market bubble in the United States quickly became a full-blown international crisis. Stock markets crashed, unemployment soared, and millions of ordinary people lost their homes, savings, and livelihoods.

Public Distrust in Banks and Governments

As the dust settled, it became clear that the people who caused the crisis—bank executives and Wall Street financiers—were not the ones bearing the consequences. Governments around the world bailed out failing banks with taxpayer money, sparking widespread outrage. The public saw this as a gross injustice: the institutions that had gambled recklessly were rescued, while ordinary citizens were left to pick up the pieces.

This injustice fueled a deep distrust in traditional financial systems. People questioned the fairness of a system that privatized profits but socialized losses. Why were banks 'too big to fail' while millions of families were deemed expendable? Why did governments prioritize rescuing financial institutions over addressing the suffering of their citizens?

The crisis also exposed the inherent weaknesses of fiat currency systems. Central banks responded to this crisis by printing vast amounts of money to stimulate the economy, leading to concerns about inflation and the devaluation of savings. For many, this raised uncomfortable questions about the long-term stability of government-backed currencies.

A Fertile Ground for Innovation

The 2008 financial crisis was more than just an economic disaster—it was a wake-up call. It revealed the vulnerabilities of centralized financial systems and the dangers of unchecked greed. It highlighted the need for alternatives—systems that have prioritized transparency, accountability, and fairness.

Out of this chaos emerged Bitcoin. The first-ever Bitcoin block, which is known as the Genesis Block, contained a poignant message: "The Times 03/Jan/2009 Chancellor on brink of second bailout for banks." That was no coincidence. Bitcoin's creator, the mysterious Satoshi Nakamoto, was making a statement—a critique of the status quo and a vision for a new kind of financial system that operated independently of banks and governments.

Bitcoin wasn't just a technological breakthrough; it was a philosophical one. It promised a decentralized system that gave power back to the individual, free from the control of centralized authorities like banks and governments. For many, it was a glimmer of hope in an era defined by mistrust and disillusionment—a chance to redefine money.

The 2008 financial crisis was not just an economic disaster. It was a seismic event that exposed the fragility of global financial systems and laid bare the systemic flaws of centralized banking. It was a moment in history that shattered trust, devastated lives, and sowed the seeds for what would become a revolutionary shift in how humanity thought about money.

The Build-Up to Disaster

The origins of the crisis can be traced back to the early 2000s when deregulation of the financial industry gave rise to unchecked risk-taking by banks. Policies encouraging homeownership, combined with aggressive lending practices, fueled a housing market boom. For years, real estate seemed like a one-way ticket to wealth. Housing prices soared, and Americans were encouraged to take on mortgages they could barely afford.

At the heart of this frenzy was the rise of subprime mortgages, loans extended to borrowers with poor credit histories. Banks, hungry for profits, packaged these risky loans into mortgage-backed securities (MBS) and sold them to investors worldwide. These securities were sliced into tranches, some of which were deemed 'safe' despite being built on a foundation of high-risk debt.

Investment banks and hedge funds amplified the problem by creating even more complex financial products, such as collateralized debt obligations (CDOs), which were essentially bundles of mortgage-backed securities. These products were sold as low-risk investments, but in reality, they were ticking time bombs.

Meanwhile, credit rating agencies—tasked with assessing the risk of these securities—gave them AAA ratings, either due to negligence, conflicts of interest, or a misunderstanding of the underlying risks. This false sense of security attracted investors ranging from pension funds to international banks, who poured billions into what they believed were safe assets.

The Spark That Ignited the Crisis

The housing market boom created a false sense of invincibility, but by 2007, cracks began to appear. Housing prices, which had risen steadily for years, started to decline. Borrowers who had taken on adjustable-rate mortgages found themselves unable to make payments as interest rates rose. Defaults surged, and the ripple effect spread quickly.

As defaults increased, the value of mortgage-backed securities and collateralized debt obligations plummeted. Financial institutions holding these assets faced catastrophic losses. What had once been considered the bedrock of the financial system now threatened its collapse.

A Global Financial Meltdown

By 2008, the crisis was in full swing. In September, Lehman Brothers, one of the oldest and largest investment banks in the United States, filed for bankruptcy. The Lehman collapse was a watershed moment, sending shockwaves through global markets. Banks stopped lending to one another, fearing insolvency, and liquidity dried up overnight.

Governments scrambled to prevent the collapse of the financial system. In the United States, Congress passed the Emergency Economic Stabilization Act, which authorized a $700 billion bailout for troubled financial institutions under the Troubled Asset Relief Program (TARP). Major banks, including Citigroup and Bank of America, were propped up with taxpayer money, while the Federal Reserve slashed interest rates and injected liquidity into the system.

In Europe, governments stepped in to rescue their own failing banks. Iceland, whose banking sector had grown exponentially in the years leading up to the crisis, saw its entire financial system collapse. The global nature of the crisis underscored the interconnectedness of modern economies and the systemic risks posed by financial institutions deemed 'too big to fail.'

The Human Cost

While governments and banks were bailed out, ordinary people bore the brunt of the crisis. In the United States alone, millions of families lost their homes to foreclosure. Unemployment rates soared as businesses shuttered, and retirement savings evaporated as stock markets crashed. The psychological toll was immense, leaving many feeling abandoned and betrayed by the very institutions that were supposed to protect them.

This stark divide—between the rescued elite and the struggling masses—fueled anger and distrust. Protests erupted worldwide, with movements like Occupy Wall Street shining a spotlight on economic inequality and corporate greed. The phrase: "*We are the 99%*" became a rallying cry for those demanding accountability and systemic change.

A Crisis of Trust

The financial crisis wasn't just about money; it was about trust—or the lack thereof. People lost faith in banks, governments, and even the concept of fiat currency itself. Central banks responded to the crisis by printing trillions of dollars to stabilize economies, leading to fears of inflation and the devaluation of savings. The cognition that a small group of institutions held so much power over the global economy was deeply unsettling.

This erosion of trust created fertile ground for alternative ideas and innovations. People began to wonder whether a better, fairer financial system was possible—one that didn't rely on central authorities prone to corruption and mismanagement.

The Seed of a Revolution

Amid this turmoil, an anonymous figure—or group—known as Satoshi Nakamoto released a whitepaper titled *'Bitcoin: A Peer-to-Peer Electronic Cash System'*. Published on October 31, 2008, this document outlined a vision for a decentralized digital currency that operated independently of banks and governments.

The timing of Bitcoin's creation was no coincidence. Satoshi Nakamoto was acutely aware of the flaws exposed by the financial crisis and sought to build a system immune to such failures.

So, Bitcoin was designed to be a form of money that couldn't be inflated, manipulated, or controlled by any single entity. It was a direct response to the failures of 2008—a tool for financial freedom in an era of widespread disillusionment.

A New Hope

The financial crisis in 2008 was a devastating event, but it also sparked a wave of innovation and introspection. It forced humanity to confront the weaknesses of traditional financing systems and consider alternatives that prioritized transparency, accountability, and individual empowerment. Bitcoin emerged not just as a technological breakthrough but as a symbol of hope—a way to rebuild trust and redefine the future of money.

This book is a continuation of that story—a journey into the heart of Bitcoin, its origins, its potential, and its promise to reshape the world. For those seeking financial freedom and a better understanding of the forces that shape our economies, the lessons of 2008 are both a warning and an inspiration.

The Birth of Bitcoin
Satoshi Nakamoto: The Visionary and the Mystery

Bitcoin's story begins with a name that has become as iconic as the invention: Satoshi Nakamoto. A figure shrouded in mystery, Satoshi is credited as the creator of Bitcoin and the author of its groundbreaking whitepaper, *'Bitcoin: A Peer-to-Peer Electronic Cash System.'* Yet, despite the revolutionary impact of their work, Satoshi's identity remains unknown—an enigma that has only deepened Bitcoin's mystique.

The Vision: A Revolution in Money

Satoshi's vision was as radical as it was elegant: to create a decentralized, peer-to-peer digital money system that operated independently of banks, governments, or any central authority. In the whitepaper released on October 31, 2008, Satoshi outlined the technical framework for Bitcoin, a currency built on blockchain technology—a transparent, immutable ledger maintained by a decentralized network of computers.

At its core, Bitcoin addressed a fundamental flaw in traditional financial systems: the need for trust. Banks act as intermediaries in financial transactions, requiring people to trust that they will act fairly and honestly. The 2008 financial crisis had shown the world just how fragile and corruptible that trust could be. Satoshi sought to eliminate this dependency by creating a system where transactions were verified not by a central authority, but by cryptographic proof.

Satoshi's whitepaper described Bitcoin as 'an electronic payment system based on cryptographic proof instead of trust.' This simple yet profound statement encapsulated the ethos of Bitcoin: transparency, security, and self-sovereignty.

The Genesis Block: A Message to the World

On January 3, 2009, Satoshi mined the first Bitcoin block, most known as the Genesis Block or Block 0. Embedded within the block's code was a message that would resonate through the ages: *"The Times 03/Jan/2009 Chancellor on brink of second bailout for banks."*

This was no random string of words. It was a deliberate timestamp referencing the headline of '*The Times*' newspaper on the day the block was mined. The message underscored the failures of the traditional banking system and framed Bitcoin as a direct response to those failures. It wasn't just a technological innovation; it was a statement of purpose.

The Genesis Block was unique in another way: the 50 bitcoins it contained could never be spent. It was a symbolic gesture, emphasizing that Bitcoin's value was not tied to any central authority or material backing, but rather to the principles of trustless security and decentralized consensus.

The Mystery: Who is Satoshi Nakamoto?

Despite being the mastermind behind one of the most transformative technologies of the 21st century, Satoshi Nakamoto has never been identified. He/she or they disappeared entirely from public view in 2011, leaving behind only a trove of cryptographic writings, forum posts, and the Bitcoin network itself.

Speculation about Satoshi's identity has run rampant. Are they an individual or a group? A cryptography expert? A disillusioned banker? A government entity? Some have suggested high-profile names, like Hal Finney (a pioneer in digital currency who was one of the first to run Bitcoin software), Nick Szabo (the creator of 'bit gold'), and even Elon Musk. Yet, none of these theories have been conclusively proven.

Satoshi's anonymity has fueled intrigue but also served a purpose. By remaining unknown, they ensured that Bitcoin could not be influenced by the biases, failures, or pressures of a single individual. Bitcoin was designed to be leaderless—a system owned by no one and accessible to everyone.

The Legacy of Satoshi's Vision

Though Satoshi Nakamoto may never be unmasked, their vision continues to inspire millions. Bitcoin has become a global movement, embodying the ideals of financial freedom, transparency, and decentralization. Satoshi's work ignited a revolution in digital currency, paving the way for countless innovations in blockchain technology and decentralized finance.

But perhaps Satoshi's greatest legacy is the question they left behind: *"What does it mean to trust a system instead of a person?"* By posing this question, Satoshi challenged the very foundations of modern finance and opened the door to a new era of economic thinking.

The Release of the Bitcoin Whitepaper

On October 31, 2008, as the world grappled with the aftermath of the global financial crisis, an email quietly made its way to a cryptography mailing list. It was from someone using the pseudonym Satoshi Nakamoto, and their subject line read: *'Bitcoin P2P e-cash paper.'* Attached was a nine-page document that would ignite a revolution: *'Bitcoin: A Peer-to-Peer Electronic Cash System.'*

This whitepaper was the blueprint for Bitcoin, a decentralized digital currency that would operate without the need for banks or governments. It wasn't the first attempt at creating digital money, but it was the first to solve a problem that had stymied previous efforts: the double-spending problem.

The Double-Spending Problem

In traditional financial systems, intermediaries like banks ensure that a digital transaction happens only once by verifying fund transfers. But in a decentralized system with no central authority, how could users trust that digital money wasn't being copied or spent twice?

Satoshi's genius lies in creating a blockchain, a distributed ledger where every transaction is recorded, timestamped, and validated by a decentralized network of computers (nodes). This innovation ensured that once a transaction was recorded on the blockchain, it could not be altered, solving the double-spending problem without needing a trusted intermediary.

Core Principles of the WhitePaper

The whitepaper outlined the fundamental principles of Bitcoin, including:

1. Decentralization: The system operates on a peer-to-peer network, eliminating the need for centralized control.
2. Scarcity: Bitcoin's supply is capped at 21 million, ensuring it remains deflationary and resistant to inflationary pressures.
3. Transparency and Security: All transactions are recorded on a public ledger, secured by cryptographic algorithms.
4. Trustless Transactions: Instead of relying on trust in a third party, Bitcoin uses mathematical proof to validate transactions.

The whitepaper described Bitcoin as 'a purely peer-to-peer version of electronic cash that would allow online payments to be sent directly from one party to another without going through a financial institution.' This simple yet revolutionary concept challenged the very foundations of traditional finance.

A Technological Masterpiece

Satoshi's whitepaper wasn't just a vision; it was a meticulously crafted technical document that combined existing technologies in innovative ways. It borrowed ideas from cryptographic pioneers like:

- David Chaum: The creator of DigiCash, one of the earliest digital currencies.
- Adam Back: The inventor of Hashcash, a proof-of-work algorithm that inspired Bitcoin's mining mechanism.
- Wei Dai: The developer of b-money, a theoretical precursor to Bitcoin.

By weaving these concepts together, Satoshi created something entirely new—a decentralized monetary system that was resilient, transparent, and virtually tamper-proof.

The Reception

Initially, the whitepaper didn't make waves. It has been shared among a niche group of cryptographers and tech enthusiasts, and some dismissed it as overly ambitious or impractical. But a few saw its potential. Among them was Hal Finney, a renowned cryptographer who became one of Bitcoin's earliest adopters and contributors.

Finney downloaded the Bitcoin software as soon as it was released and was engaged in discussions with Satoshi about refining and improving the system. His early involvement helped shape the practical implementation of Bitcoin's theoretical framework.

A Revolutionary Foundation

The release of the Bitcoin whitepaper was more than just a technical milestone; it was the beginning of a movement. Satoshi's vision wasn't merely to create a new form of money but to offer an alternative to a broken financial system—a way for individuals to regain control over their wealth in a world dominated by centralized institutions.

The timing of the whitepaper's release—just weeks after the collapse of Lehman Brothers and the start of massive government bailouts—was no coincidence. It was a direct response to the failings of traditional finance and a call to rethink how value could be stored and transferred in the digital age.

Today, the Bitcoin whitepaper is celebrated as one of the most influential documents in the history of technology and finance. Its nine pages have sparked an entire industry, reshaped global economies, and inspired countless innovations in blockchain technology.

As we move forward in this book, we'll explore how this bold idea evolved from a simple whitepaper into a global phenomenon, transforming the way we think about money, trust, and freedom.

The Whitepaper of Bitcoin is available in several languages at https://bitcoin.org/en/bitcoin-paper

The Mining of the Genesis Block and Its Embedded Message

On January 3, 2009, a silent revolution began. As we saw earlier in this book, Satoshi Nakamoto, the mysterious creator of Bitcoin, mined the first-ever block of the Bitcoin blockchain. Known as the Genesis Block or Block 0, this event marked the birth of a decentralized monetary system that would challenge traditional financial paradigms and ignite a global movement.

What is the Genesis Block?

The Genesis Block is the foundational block of the Bitcoin blockchain. It is where it all began—a single block of transactions that set the stage for every Bitcoin mined and every transaction validated since.

Unlike subsequent blocks, the Genesis Block has unique properties:

- Its 50 BTC reward cannot be spent, making it purely symbolic.

- It is hard-coded into Bitcoin's software, serving as the immutable cornerstone of the blockchain.

The Embedded Message: A Critique of the System

Embedded within the Genesis Block was a powerful and deliberate statement:

"The Times 03/Jan/2009 Chancellor on brink of second bailout for banks."

This message referenced the headline of *'The Times'* newspaper on the day the block was mined. At first glance, it served as a timestamp to prove the block's creation date. But its deeper meaning was unmistakable—it was a critique of the traditional financial system, a system that had failed spectacularly in the 2008 financial crisis.

The reference to bank bailouts highlighted Satoshi's dissatisfaction with a world where governments and central banks printed money to rescue failing financial institutions, leaving taxpayers to bear the cost. This embedded message was not just a technical detail; it was a manifesto. It underscored the motivation behind Bitcoin: to create a monetary system that couldn't be manipulated or debased by centralized powers.

How the Genesis Block Was Mined

Mining the Genesis Block wasn't just the start of Bitcoin; it was the launch of an entirely new technological framework. Here's how it unfolded:

1. Proof of Work: Satoshi used Bitcoin's proof-of-work algorithm to solve a cryptographic puzzle, validating the block and securing it on the blockchain.

2. Network Creation: With the mining of the Genesis Block, Bitcoin's decentralized network was established, though, at this point, Satoshi was the sole participant.

3. Unspendable Reward: The 50 BTC mined with the Genesis Block could never be spent, emphasizing that Bitcoin's value was not tied to its creator but to the integrity of its decentralized system.

Symbolism and Significance

The Genesis Block is rich with symbolism. It represents:

- A New Beginning: In a world disillusioned by financial corruption, it offered an alternative based on transparency and mathematical certainty.
- Independence: By mining the first block, Satoshi set the precedent for a system that operates without reliance on central authorities.
- Community Ownership: From the Genesis Block onward, Bitcoin's network was designed to be maintained and validated by its users, not controlled by a single entity.

Early Reactions

At the time, the Genesis Block went largely unnoticed. The world was still reeling from the financial crisis, and few outside niche cryptography circles paid attention to Bitcoin. But for those who did, the Genesis Block and its embedded message were profound. It wasn't just the start of a new technology; it was the start of a movement.

Cryptographer Hal Finney was one of the first to recognize the significance of the Genesis Block. He downloaded Bitcoin's software and mined early blocks alongside Satoshi, helping to validate the system and lay the groundwork for its future.

The Legacy of the Genesis Block

Today, the Genesis Block stands as a historical milestone. It is more than just data on a blockchain; it is a symbol of resistance against centralized control and a testament to the power of decentralization. Every block mined since builds on its foundation, a reminder of Bitcoin's origins and its enduring purpose.

Satoshi Nakamoto's decision to embed that message was both a critique and a rallying cry. It signaled the birth of a financial system designed to empower individuals, free from the constraints of traditional banking. For millions of Bitcoin enthusiasts around the world, the Genesis Block remains a source of inspiration—a reminder that from the ashes of a crisis, innovation can rise.

As we continue this journey through Bitcoin's story, the Genesis Block serves as a guiding light, reminding us of the ideals that shaped its creation: transparency, fairness, and the unyielding pursuit of financial freedom.

Part 2. How Bitcoin Works

What is Blockchain?

Imagine you're writing in a notebook that everyone can see, but no one can erase or change what has been written. That's essentially what a blockchain is—a digital ledger that records information in a way that is transparent, secure, and permanent.

But let's break it down step by step.

The Basics of Blockchain

A blockchain is a system for recording information in a series of blocks. These blocks are like pages in a digital book, where each page contains a set of records (transactions, data, or other information). Once a page is full, it's locked, time-stamped, and linked to the next page. Together, these pages form a 'chain' of blocks, hence the term blockchain.

Key characteristics:

1. Distributed: Instead of being stored in one central place, the blockchain exists on thousands of computers (called nodes) worldwide.

2. Immutable: Once information is added to a block, it cannot be altered or deleted.

3. Transparent: Anyone can view the blockchain and see what has been recorded.

How Blockchain Works

Here's how a blockchain operates, step by step:
1. Data Creation: Someone initiates an action, like sending Bitcoin or recording a contract. This action creates data that needs to be added to the blockchain.
2. Verification: The network of computers (nodes) checks the action to ensure it's valid. For example, if you send Bitcoin, the network verifies that you have enough Bitcoin to send.
3. Block Formation: Once verified, the data is grouped into a block along with other transactions.
4. Consensus: Before the block can be added to the blockchain, the network must agree that it's legitimate. This process is called consensus.
5. Block Addition: Once consensus is reached, the block is added to the blockchain, linked to the previous block. This link is secured by cryptographic hashing (more on that soon).
6. Permanent Record: The new block is now part of the chain, and its data cannot be changed.

What Makes Blockchain Special?

1. Decentralization: Unlike traditional systems (like banks) where a central authority controls everything, blockchain operates on a network of computers. No single person or organization owns it, making it more secure and democratic.
2. Security Through Cryptography:
   - Each block is secured with a cryptographic hash, a unique digital fingerprint created from the block's data.
   - Even a tiny change in the data would completely alter the hash, immediately alerting the network to tampering.
   - This makes the blockchain tamper-proof.
3. Transparency: Because the blockchain is public, anyone can view the records. This transparency builds trust, as no one can secretly change the data.
4. Immutability: Once data is recorded, it cannot be changed. This permanence ensures that the blockchain's records are reliable and trustworthy.

An Analogy for Simplicity

Think of a blockchain as a digital version of a chain of receipts:

- Each receipt (block) contains a list of purchases (transactions).
- Once a receipt is written, it's stamped and locked.
- The next receipt is linked to the previous one by including its stamp (hash).
- This chain of receipts grows over time, forming a complete, unchangeable history.

Decentralization in Action

Here is why decentralization matters:

- In traditional systems, if the central authority (like a bank) was hacked, the entire system was compromised.
- In blockchain, there's no central point of failure. The ledger exists across thousands of nodes, making it nearly impossible to hack or corrupt.

Bitcoin's Blockchain: The First of Its Kind

The Bitcoin blockchain is the original blockchain, and it was designed specifically for Bitcoin transactions. Here's what makes it unique:

- Limited Supply: Bitcoin's blockchain ensures that only 21 million bitcoins will ever exist, making it deflationary.
- Proof of Work: Bitcoin uses mining to validate transactions and add them to the blockchain. It involves solving complex mathematical puzzles and ensuring security and fairness.
- Transparency and Pseudonymity: While transactions are visible to everyone, users remain pseudonymous, identified only by their wallet addresses.

Applications Beyond Bitcoin

Although blockchain was invented for Bitcoin, its uses go far beyond cryptocurrency. It can be applied to:

- Supply Chain Management: Tracking goods from production to delivery.
- Healthcare: Securing patient records.
- Voting Systems: Ensuring transparent and tamper-proof elections.
- Smart Contracts: Automating agreements without intermediaries.

Challenges of Blockchain

While revolutionary, blockchain isn't perfect:

1. Scalability: Current blockchains like Bitcoin can handle only a limited number of transactions per second.
2. Energy Use: The mining process in proof-of-work systems consumes significant electricity.
3. Complexity: For many, the technology is still difficult to understand, limiting widespread adoption.

The Foundation of Trust

Blockchain is more than a technology; it's a paradigm shift. It replaces trust in institutions with trust in mathematics, enabling systems that are fairer, more transparent, and more secure. For Bitcoin, blockchain is its backbone—a decentralized ledger that ensures every transaction is valid, every user is accountable, and every bitcoin is unique.

As we explore Bitcoin further, understanding blockchain is key to appreciating why this system transforms how we think about money, ownership, and trust.

Mining and Proof of Work: The Heartbeat of Bitcoin

Bitcoin mining is the process that keeps the Bitcoin network secure, decentralized, and functional. It's the backbone of Bitcoin's blockchain, where new bitcoins are created and transactions validated. But what makes mining special is its reliance on a concept called Proof of Work (PoW)—a system that ensures fairness, security, and decentralization through computational effort.

Let's break it down so anyone can understand.

What is Bitcoin Mining?

Mining is the process by which computers (better known as miners) compete to solve complex mathematical puzzles. When a miner solves the puzzle, they:

1. Add a new block of transactions to the blockchain.

2. Earn a reward as newly minted bitcoins (and transaction fees).

Just think of miners as accountants who maintain Bitcoin's public ledger (the blockchain). But instead of being chosen or hired, miners earn the right to update the ledger by solving cryptographic puzzles faster than anyone else.

How Does Mining Work?

Here's a step-by-step explanation of the mining process:

1. Transaction Pool: When someone sends Bitcoin, the transaction is broadcast to the network and placed in a pool of unconfirmed transactions (called the mempool).
2. Block Formation: Miners gather these unconfirmed transactions and package them into a block. Just think of that block as a digital container holding multiple transactions.
3. Proof of Work Puzzle:
   - To add the block to the blockchain, miners must solve a cryptographic puzzle.

- This puzzle involves finding a specific number (called a nonce) that, when combined with the block's data, produces a hash—a unique string of characters that meets specific conditions.
- The hash must begin with a certain number of zeros, making it extremely difficult to find but easy to verify.

4. Competition Among Miners:
   - Miners use specialized hardware to generate billions of guesses per second to find the correct nonce.
   - The first miner to solve the puzzle broadcasts their solution to the network.

5. Validation and Reward:
   - The network validates the solution. If it's correct, the block is added to the blockchain.
   - The winning miner receives the block reward (currently 6.25 BTC as of 2024) and transaction fees from the block's transactions.

What is Proof of Work?

Proof of Work (PoW) is the mechanism that makes mining possible. It's a system where miners must perform computational work (solving the puzzle) to validate transactions and add blocks to the blockchain. Here's why it's important:

1. Security: PoW makes it extremely difficult and expensive to alter the blockchain. Changing even a single block would require re-mining all subsequent blocks, which is virtually impossible for any attacker.

2. Decentralization: PoW ensures no single miner or group can control the network. Mining power is distributed globally, making the system resilient to censorship or manipulation.

3. Fairness: PoW rewards miners based on their effort and computational power, creating an open and competitive process.

Why Mining Matters

Mining does more than create new bitcoins—it's essential for the network's health:

1. Transaction Validation: Miners ensure that Bitcoin transactions are legitimate and prevent double-spending.

2. Network Security: By requiring immense computational effort, PoW protects the blockchain from attacks.

3. Decentralization: Mining allows anyone with the proper hardware to participate, keeping the network open and permissionless.

The Role of Hashing in Mining

At the core of Bitcoin mining is a process called hashing:

- A hash is a fixed-length string of characters that represents data.

- Bitcoin uses the SHA-256 algorithm, which takes any input and generates a 256-bit hash.

- Even a tiny change in the input completely changes the hash, making it impossible to predict.

Miners use hashing to find the correct nonce for their block, ensuring it meets the network's difficulty requirements.

Challenges of Mining

1. Energy Consumption:

   Mining requires enormous amounts of electricity, leading to concerns about its environmental impact.
   However, many miners are adopting renewable energy sources to reduce their carbon footprint.

2. Rising Difficulty:

   As more miners join the network, the difficulty of solving the cryptographic puzzle increases. This ensures that blocks are mined roughly every 10 minutes, maintaining a consistent supply of new bitcoins.

3. Cost of Equipment:

   Mining requires specialized hardware (ASICs) that can cost thousands of dollars, making it less accessible for individuals.

Mining Rewards: The Bitcoin Incentive

Miners are rewarded for their work with two types of incentives:

1. Block Rewards: Newly minted bitcoins given to the miner who solves the puzzle. This reward halves approximately every four years (Bitcoin halving), reducing the rate of new Bitcoin issuance.

2. Transaction Fees: Fees paid by users to prioritize their transactions. As block rewards decrease over time, transaction fees will become the primary incentive for miners.

Proof of Work vs. Alternatives

While Proof of Work is the backbone of Bitcoin, other cryptocurrencies use alternative mechanisms like Proof of Stake (PoS). Here's why Bitcoin sticks to PoW:

- Proven Security: PoW has been battle-tested since Bitcoin's creation in 2009, making it the most secure consensus mechanism.

- Fair Distribution: PoW ensures Bitcoin is earned through work, not pre-distributed or influenced by wealth.

The Significance of Mining

Bitcoin mining is more than just a technical process; it's a system that embodies Bitcoin's core values:
- Transparency: Every transaction is visible to the entire network.
- Fairness: Anyone can participate in mining, reinforcing Bitcoin's open and decentralized nature.
- Security: Mining makes Bitcoin resilient against fraud, censorship, and manipulation.

The Future of Mining

As Bitcoin evolves, so does mining:
- Sustainability: Innovations in renewable energy are making mining greener.
- Economic Shifts: As block rewards diminish, transaction fees will play a bigger role in incentivizing miners.
- Global Reach: Mining remains a global industry, with participants from all corners of the Earth contributing to Bitcoin's security.

Conclusion: The Lifeblood of Bitcoin

Mining and Proof of Work are the lifeblood of the Bitcoin network. They ensure that Bitcoin remains decentralized, secure, and functional, fulfilling Satoshi Nakamoto's vision of a financial system without trust in intermediaries. While mining has challenges, its role in maintaining Bitcoin's integrity is irreplaceable—a testament to the genius of Bitcoin's design.

Mining and Proof of Work: A Path to Profit

Bitcoin mining isn't just the backbone of the Bitcoin network—it's also a potentially profitable activity for individuals and businesses. The miners are rewarded with Bitcoin by contributing computational power to validate transactions and secure the blockchain. For those who approach it strategically, mining can be both a way to support the network and a lucrative venture.

Bitcoin Mining as a Profit Opportunity

At its core, Bitcoin mining is an economic activity. Miners are compensated for their efforts with two sources of income:

1. Block Rewards: Newly minted bitcoins for each block mined. As of 2024, the reward is 6.25 BTC per block, but this amount decreases over time due to the halving.
2. Transaction Fees: Payments from users for processing transactions. These fees will grow in importance as block rewards decline.

If managed correctly, mining can generate significant revenue, making it appealing to individuals and businesses alike.

What It Takes to Mine Bitcoin Profitably

While the concept is straightforward, mining profitably requires careful planning, knowledge, and strategic investments. Here's what you need to consider:

1. Electricity Costs:
   Electricity is the highest expense in mining. Miners consume large amounts of energy to power specialized equipment, so reducing electricity costs is crucial for profitability.

   Strategies for Lowering Costs:
   - Geographical Advantage: Establish mining operations in regions with abundant, low-cost energy sources, such as hydropower.
   - Renewable Energy: Many miners use solar, wind, or hydroelectric power, which can significantly reduce costs and improve sustainability.
   - Government Incentives: Some countries or regions offer subsidies or tax breaks for renewable energy usage.

2. Tax Optimization:
   Understanding local tax laws is key to maximizing profits. Some regions offer low or zero taxes for cryptocurrency mining operations.

Tax-Free Zones:
- Countries like El Salvador, Ethiopia, and Kenya have created crypto-friendly environments with minimal or no mining taxes.
- Establishing operations in regions with favorable tax policies can significantly impact your bottom line.

Keep meticulous records of expenses and earnings for tax reporting and deductions.

3. Efficient Mining Equipment:
   - Mining profitability depends heavily on the efficiency of your hardware.
   - ASIC Miners (Application-Specific Integrated Circuits) are the gold standard for Bitcoin mining. They are optimized for the SHA-256 algorithm and deliver high computational power with lower energy consumption.
   - Regularly upgrading equipment to more efficient models can reduce operational costs and boost profitability.

4. Economies of Scale:
   Larger operations gain advantages such as bulk discounts on equipment, energy contracts, and maintenance. Pooling resources with other miners or running a mining farm can increase profitability.

5. Mining Pools:
   For individuals, joining a mining pool—a group of miners combining their computational power—can provide a steady income stream. Sharing rewards among participants reduces the uncertainty associated with solo mining.

6. Environmental Impact:
   Many miners are addressing concerns about energy consumption by adopting green mining strategies. Utilizing renewable energy not only lowers costs but also aligns

operations with sustainability goals, improving public
perception and regulatory compliance.

7. Monitoring Bitcoin Price:
   Mining profitability depends heavily on Bitcoin's market price.
   A rising Bitcoin price can make mining more lucrative, while a
   falling price requires miners to optimize costs even further.

Mining as a Business

For those with capital and expertise, mining can evolve into a
full-fledged business. Here's how:

- Setting Up Mining Farms:
  - A mining farm involves deploying multiple ASIC miners
    in a facility optimized for cooling, energy efficiency, and
    security.
  - Mining farms can scale operations to maximize
    profitability and take advantage of bulk pricing for
    equipment and electricity.

- Hosting Services:
  Some mining businesses offer hosting services, allowing
  individuals to rent space and resources for their equipment.

- Diversifying Income Streams:
  Beyond mining, businesses can explore related opportunities,
  such as selling mining hardware, offering consulting services,
  or developing software for mining optimization.

The Challenges of Mining Profitably

While mining can be profitable, it's not without its challenges:

- Initial Investment: High-quality mining equipment and
  infrastructure require significant upfront costs.
- Market Volatility: Bitcoin's price fluctuations can impact mining
  profitability, especially during bear markets.
- Competition: Mining difficulty increases as more participants
  join the network, reducing the likelihood of earning rewards.

- Regulatory Risks: Changes in government policies or regulations can affect operations, particularly in regions where crypto mining is restricted.

Mining Strategies for Long-Term Success

1. Research and Planning:
   Analyze the local energy market, tax policies, and regulatory conditions carefully before establishing operations.

   Use profitability calculators to estimate potential returns based on electricity costs, hardware efficiency, and Bitcoin's price.

2. Adopt Energy-Efficient Practices:
   Invest in energy-efficient cooling systems to reduce operational costs.

   Explore partnerships with renewable energy providers for long-term savings.

3. Diversify Revenue:
   Combine mining with other crypto-related ventures to mitigate risks and increase income streams.

4. Stay Adaptable:
   The crypto space evolves rapidly. Successful miners stay informed about industry trends, new technologies, and market dynamics to remain competitive.

Mining as Profit and Purpose

Bitcoin mining isn't just about earning rewards—it's about supporting the network and contributing to the decentralized revolution. For those willing to invest the time, effort, and resources, mining can be a profitable venture with significant potential for growth. Leveraging low electricity costs, favorable tax policies, and efficient equipment enables miners to transform this technical process into a lucrative business or a stable source of personal income.

Whether you're an individual with a single mining rig or a business running a large-scale operation, Bitcoin mining represents an opportunity to participate in one of the most transformative technologies of our time while earning real financial rewards.

My $2,000,000 Bitcoin Mining Business

In May 2023, I founded Bitmern Mining, a business that became one of my most successful ventures, currently valued at over $2,000,000.00. While I initially started mining operations in the United Arab Emirates (UAE), I later expanded and relocated my business to Ethiopia, which has proven to be one of the best locations for Bitcoin mining due to its low electricity costs and crypto-friendly environment.

Bitmern Mining was founded with a clear vision: to build a profitable Bitcoin mining operation by leveraging strategic locations and adopting efficient practices. I started mining in the UAE, where I benefited from a stable and business-friendly environment. However, I recognized that in order to scale the operation, I needed a location with lower operational costs and more favorable mining conditions.

That's when I moved the core of my operations to Ethiopia. The country offered several advantages:

- Low Electricity Costs: A significant reduction in energy expenses, the largest cost factor in Bitcoin mining.
- Crypto-Friendly Policies: As of the time of writing this book, Ethiopia's regulatory environment is supportive of Bitcoin

mining, enabling operations to thrive without unnecessary interference.

Relocating Bitmern Mining to Ethiopia was a strategic decision that allowed me to optimize costs while increasing profitability. However, as with any location, it's important to remain vigilant, as regulatory environments can shift over time.

Strategies Behind My Success

Running a Bitcoin mining business is more than just plugging in machines and letting them work—it requires careful planning, ongoing research, and intelligent strategies. Here's how I've made Bitmern Mining a success:

1. Geographical Optimization:
    Mining in Ethiopia benefited me from lower electricity costs, drastically reducing operational expenses.
    Choosing regions with abundant energy resources, such as hydropower, has also contributed to sustainability and cost-efficiency.

2. Market Awareness and Price Targets:
    One of the simplest yet most effective strategies I've used is setting price targets for the Bitcoin I mine.
    For example, I decide at what price I will sell portions of my mined Bitcoin to lock in profits, ensuring I capitalize on market opportunities rather than reacting emotionally to volatility.

3. The Power of Holding (HODLing):
    While selling mined Bitcoin at specific targets is one strategy, I also embrace HODLing—holding onto Bitcoin for long-term appreciation. By combining both approaches, I've balanced short-term profitability with long-term gains.

4. Scaling Operations:
    I've reinvested profits back into the business to scale operations. That includes acquiring more efficient mining

equipment, such as ASICs (Application-Specific Integrated Circuits), to stay competitive in an industry where technology evolves rapidly.

5. Adaptability:
   Bitcoin mining is dynamic, with changing market conditions, difficulty adjustments, and energy costs. Staying adaptable has been critical to my business's success.

Why Mining Has Been My Best Investment

Mining Bitcoin is a business that requires strategic thinking and a willingness to adapt. Since I started mining when Bitcoin was priced at $25,000, I've witnessed the benefits of carefully managing operational costs and market strategies. Bitmern Mining has not only provided a steady income stream but has also allowed me to participate directly in the Bitcoin ecosystem, supporting the network while generating significant returns.

For me, this journey has been the best investment I've ever made, combining my passion for Bitcoin with a business model that thrives based on innovation and strategic thinking.

More about Bitmern Mining at the QR Code below:

Challenging Central Banking and Fiat Currencies

For centuries, centralized systems like banks and governments have dominated the global financial ecosystem. They dictate the supply of money, regulate its flow, and influence the economic policies that shape everyday life. Bitcoin, however, poses a direct challenge to this status quo—a revolutionary alternative aiming to redefine how money operates in the modern world.

The Role of Central Banks and Fiat Currencies

To understand Bitcoin's challenge, we must first examine the traditional financial system. At its core are central banks, institutions responsible for:

1. Issuing Currency: Central banks control the supply of money, deciding how much to print and inject into the economy.
2. Regulating Inflation: Central banks adjust interest rates and the money supply to stabilize the economy and manage inflation.
3. Monetary Policy: Central banks set policies that influence credit, borrowing, and economic growth.

The currency issued by central banks, referred to as fiat money, holds no intrinsic value. Unlike gold or other commodities, fiat money derives value from trust in the government that backs it. This system has been the foundation of global finance since the abandonment of the gold standard in the 20th century.

Bitcoin: A Decentralized Alternative

Bitcoin challenges the very foundations of the traditional financial system. Here's how:

1. Decentralization:

   Unlike fiat currencies, which are issued and controlled by central banks, Bitcoin operates on a decentralized network. No single authority has control over its supply or transactions.

This eliminates the dangers of centralization, such as corruption, poor management, or excessive control by a governing body.

2. Fixed Supply:

   Central banks can print unlimited amounts of money, leading to inflation and the erosion of purchasing power. Bitcoin, however, has a hard cap of 21 million coins. This scarcity ensures that Bitcoin cannot be devalued through excessive issuance.

3. Borderless and Permissionless:

   Traditional financial systems depend on intermediaries like banks to process transactions, often resulting in fees, delays, and restrictions. In contrast, Bitcoin transactions are peer-to-peer, requiring no intermediaries, making them borderless and accessible to anyone with an internet connection.

4. Trustless System:

   Central banking relies on trust in institutions to act in the public's best interest. Bitcoin eliminates the need for trust by using cryptographic proof and a decentralized consensus mechanism. Transactions are verified by the network, not by a central authority.

5. Resistance to Censorship:

   Governments and banks have the authority to freeze accounts, block payments, or restrict access to funds. In contrast, Bitcoin is censorship-resistant, meaning no entity can unilaterally block a transaction.

How Bitcoin Challenges Central Banking

1. Monetary Policy:

    - Central banks use monetary policy to manipulate economic conditions, often leading to unintended consequences such as inflation or asset bubbles.
    - Bitcoin's monetary policy is pre-determined and transparent, governed by code rather than human intervention. Its supply schedule is fixed, with new bitcoins released at a decreasing rate through mining rewards (halvings).

2. Inflation Control:

    - Central banks often print money to stimulate the economy, but this practice can lead to hyperinflation in severe cases (e.g., Zimbabwe, and Venezuela).
    - Bitcoin, with its fixed supply, is inherently deflationary. As demand grows and supply remains capped, Bitcoin's value is likely to increase over time.

3. Financial Inclusion:

    - The traditional financial system leaves billions of people excluded, particularly those without access to banks or credit. Bitcoin offers a banking alternative for the unbanked, allowing anyone to store, send, and receive money without needing a bank account.

4. Global Reserve Currency:

    - Fiat currencies like the U.S. dollar dominate global trade, giving the issuing country immense power. Bitcoin offers a global, neutral alternative—a currency that isn't tied to any one nation or political system.

Challenges Bitcoin Poses to Fiat Currencies

1. Loss of Monetary Control:

   Governments depend on their control of the money supply to manage economies. Bitcoin's decentralized nature removes this power, limiting their capacity to intervene in economic crises.

2. Erosion of Trust in Fiat:

   As Bitcoin grows in adoption, it highlights the weaknesses of fiat currencies, particularly in countries suffering from economic mismanagement or corruption. Citizens increasingly turn to Bitcoin as a hedge against failing fiat systems.

3. Competition with Central Bank Digital Currencies (CBDCs):

   In response to Bitcoin, many governments are exploring CBDCs—digital versions of fiat currencies. While these might incorporate blockchain technology, they retain the centralized control Bitcoin seeks to eliminate.

Bitcoin as a Financial Revolution

Bitcoin's challenge to traditional finance isn't just technological—it's philosophical. It questions the very need for centralized control over money and proposes a new paradigm where:

- Individuals, not institutions, control their wealth.
- Transparency replaces opacity.
- Mathematical certainty replaces human discretion.

By offering an alternative to central banking and fiat currencies, Bitcoin represents a financial revolution—a shift from trust in authorities to trust in technology.

Comparison of inflation, scarcity, and trust

Bitcoin and fiat currencies differ in their fundamental approach to inflation, scarcity, and trust. These differences aren't just technical—they shape the way wealth is stored, transferred, and valued.

Inflation: The Erosion of Value

Fiat Currencies: Built for Inflation

Inflation is the gradual increase in prices over time, which reduces the purchasing power of money. For fiat currencies, inflation is an expected outcome, as central banks often increase the money supply to stimulate economic growth or respond to crises.

While moderate inflation can be a sign of a healthy economy, excessive inflation erodes wealth and can destabilize economies.

Examples of Fiat Inflation:

1. Hyperinflation in Zimbabwe and Venezuela:
   - In Zimbabwe, during the late 2000s, hyperinflation reached unimaginable levels, with prices doubling every 24 hours. The country's currency lost so much value that it was replaced by foreign currencies, such as the U.S. dollar.
   - In Venezuela, hyperinflation peaked at over 1,000,000% in 2018, wiping out the savings of millions and plunging the nation into economic chaos.
2. The U.S. Dollar:
   - Even the world's reserve currency, the U.S. dollar, hasn't escaped the effects of inflation. Over the past 100 years, the dollar has lost approximately 90–96% of its purchasing power.
   - For example, what you could buy with $1 in 1920 would cost $26 today. This gradual erosion, though less dramatic than hyperinflation, illustrates how fiat

currencies lose value over time due to policies such as quantitative easing and deficit spending.

3. The Euro:
   - Since its introduction in 1999, the Euro has also lost value due to inflation. By some estimates, the Euro has lost approximately 35–40% of its purchasing power since its inception, making it less effective as a store of value over two decades.

Bitcoin: Designed to Resist Inflation

By design, Bitcoin is deflationary, with a supply limit of 21 million coins. This prevents any central authority from arbitrarily increasing its supply.

Unlike fiat currencies, Bitcoin's issuance rate decreases over time due to the halving mechanism, which cuts the number of new bitcoins entering circulation roughly every four years.

This fixed supply and predictable issuance schedule make Bitcoin inherently resistant to inflation. Over time, as demand increases and supply remains capped, Bitcoin's value is more likely to appreciate than depreciate.

Scarcity: The Value of Limitation

Fiat Currencies: Unlimited Supply

Fiat currencies are not scarce; central banks can print unlimited amounts to address economic needs. While this flexibility can help stabilize economies during crises, it also leads to currency devaluation and inflation.

For example, during the 2020 COVID-19 pandemic, governments worldwide printed trillions of dollars to support economies, significantly increasing the money supply and sparking concerns about long-term inflation.

Bitcoin: Digital Scarcity

Bitcoin's supply is permanently capped at 21 million coins, creating digital scarcity. This scarcity mirrors the physical limitations of gold but with added advantages:

- Bitcoin is simpler to store, transfer, and verify.
- Its supply is fully transparent, as anyone can audit the blockchain to confirm the total number of bitcoins in existence.

Economic Implications of Scarcity

Bitcoin's scarcity positions it as a store of value, often referred to as 'digital gold.' In contrast, fiat currencies serve as mediums of exchange but fail to preserve long-term value due to their unlimited supply.

Trust: The Foundation of Value

Fiat Currencies: Trust in Institutions

Fiat currencies derive their value from trust in governments and central banks. People accept fiat because they believe in the stability of these institutions and their capacity to regulate the economy.

However, this trust can be fragile and eroded by:

- Poor Economic Policies: Irresponsible decisions, such as excessive debt or hyperinflation, weaken confidence in fiat.
- Centralized Power: Governments and banks are authorized to freeze accounts, seize funds, or manipulate the money supply, raising concerns about misuse.
- Lack of Transparency: Central banks operate behind closed doors, leaving the public unaware of the full scope of their actions.

Bitcoin: Trust in Technology

Bitcoin eliminates the need for trust in central authorities by relying on cryptographic proof and decentralized consensus.

Its design ensures transparency and predictability:

- Open Ledger: Every transaction is logged on a public blockchain, which is accessible to anyone.
- Immutable Rules: Bitcoin's monetary policy is embedded in its code, ensuring it cannot be modified by any entity.
- Decentralization: No single organization or government controls Bitcoin, reducing the risk of corruption or censorship.

The Shift in Trust

Bitcoin represents a paradigm shift from trusting human institutions to trusting mathematical systems. For individuals in countries with unstable economies or authoritarian governments, this shift is particularly appealing.

Summary Comparison Table

Aspect	Fiat Currencies	Bitcoin
Inflation	Unlimited supply leads to inflation and currency erosion	Fixed supply ensures deflationary pressure over time
Scarcity	No inherent scarcity; supply can be increased at will	Hard cap of 21 million coins creates digital scarcity
Trust	Relies on governments, central banks, and institutions	Relies on cryptographic proof and decentralized systems

The Bigger Picture

Bitcoin's resistance to inflation, digital scarcity, and trustworthy operation make it a transformative alternative to fiat currencies. While fiat systems dominate as mediums of exchange, Bitcoin's strengths lie in preserving wealth, offering financial sovereignty, and challenging the centralized control of money.

By addressing the weaknesses of fiat currencies, Bitcoin positions itself not just as a technological innovation but as a movement for economic empowerment and financial freedom.

What is Bitcoin Based On?

Bitcoin is frequently described as a revolutionary technology, but its foundation goes far beyond just code and cryptography. Financially, Bitcoin represents a paradigm shift in how we think about money, value, and trust. Unlike traditional currencies, which rely on governments and institutions, Bitcoin's financial system is based on mathematical certainty, scarcity, and decentralization.

Let's break down the financial foundations of Bitcoin.

1. Scarcity: The Power of Limited Supply

At the heart of Bitcoin's value is its scarcity. Modeled after gold, as written above, Bitcoin has a fixed supply of 21 million coins, ensuring that no more can ever be created. This limitation makes Bitcoin deflationary, unlike fiat currencies, which can be printed in unlimited quantities by central banks.

Economic Principles of Scarcity:
- Scarcity drives value. Just as gold has been prized for its rarity, Bitcoin's finite nature makes it an attractive store of value.
- As demand rises and supply remains constant, Bitcoin's value is projected to increase over time.

Comparison with Fiat:
- Fiat currencies lose value over time due to inflation and uncontrolled money printing. In contrast, Bitcoin's scarcity protects it from devaluation, making it a reliable hedge against inflation.

2. Decentralization: Trust Through Distributed Systems

Financially, Bitcoin is built on the principle of decentralization, which eliminates the need for intermediaries like banks or governments to validate and control transactions.

Why Decentralization Matters:
- No Central Authority: Bitcoin's value isn't tied to the policies of a single government or institution, making it immune to monetary mismanagement or corruption.
- Global Accessibility: Anyone with an internet connection can participate in the Bitcoin network, giving it a universal appeal.

Economic Impact:
- Decentralization reduces systemic risks, such as the collapse of a single institution that could destabilize an entire economy.
- It empowers individuals by granting them full control over their wealth, free from third-party interference.

3. Utility: Medium of Exchange and Store of Value

Bitcoin derives financial value from its utility as both a medium of exchange and a store of value.

Medium of Exchange:
- Bitcoin allows for peer-to-peer transactions without intermediaries, enabling fast, borderless payments.
- Its adoption by merchants and businesses is growing, providing real-world use cases as a currency.

Store of Value:
- Bitcoin's scarcity, security, and resistance to inflation make it a reliable store of value, often called digital gold.
- Investors view Bitcoin as a hedge against economic uncertainty and a way to preserve wealth over time.

4. Security: Trust in the Network

Bitcoin's financial integrity is based on its trustless security model, which uses cryptographic algorithms and decentralized consensus to ensure its reliability.

Key Features:

- Transactions are verified through a network of miners and nodes, making fraud or double-spending nearly impossible.

- The blockchain's transparency allows anyone to audit the network, fostering trust without requiring intermediaries.

Economic Implications:

- Unlike fiat systems, where trust in central banks or governments can be misplaced, Bitcoin's value is grounded in its mathematical certainty and technological robustness.

5. Market Adoption: Network Effects

Bitcoin's financial value is strongly influenced by its adoption rate. As more individuals, businesses, and institutions adopt and invest in Bitcoin, its value grows stronger through network effects.

Economic Concept:

- The more people use Bitcoin, the more valuable it becomes. This self-reinforcing cycle increases demand and trust in the system.

Institutional Adoption:

- Large institutions like Tesla, MicroStrategy, and investment funds have added Bitcoin to their balance sheets, further legitimizing its role as a financial asset.

- Central banks and governments are increasingly paying attention, with some incorporating Bitcoin into their national reserves.

6. Speculation and Perception

Financially, Bitcoin's value is also influenced by market speculation and public perception.

Speculation:
- Bitcoin is traded globally, and its price often reflects market sentiment, geopolitical events, and macroeconomic trends.

- Speculators play a significant role in driving short-term volatility, which can also create profit opportunities.

Perception:
- Bitcoin is increasingly regarded as a reliable hedge against inflation, a safe haven asset, and an innovative financial instrument. This perception contributes to its growing value.

7. Comparison to Traditional Assets

Bitcoin's financial foundation makes it comparable to, but distinct from, traditional assets like gold and fiat currencies.

Aspect	Bitcoin	Gold	Fiat Currencies
Scarcity	Hard cap of 21 million coins	Limited but not fixed	Unlimited supply
Portability	Easily transferred digitally worldwide	Physical and cumbersome	Physical but lightweight
Inflation	Deflationary by design	Inflation-resistant	Prone to inflation
Transparency	Fully auditable on blockchain	Not fully transparent	Limited transparency

8. Independence from Geopolitical Risks

Bitcoin is financially based on its neutrality:

- It is not tied to any government, making it resistant to sanctions, political instability, or currency devaluations.
- This independence is particularly appealing in regions experiencing economic turmoil, where people turn to Bitcoin as a stable alternative.

9. The Psychological Shift: Money of the People

Bitcoin's financial value is also rooted in its role as a symbol of economic sovereignty. It empowers individuals to manage their wealth without relying on traditional systems.

- Ownership and Control:
  Bitcoin holders have control over their assets through private keys. There's no need to rely on banks or trust third parties.

- A Movement for Change:
  Bitcoin's appeal lies not just in its functionality but in its ethos of decentralization, transparency, and freedom from traditional financial constraints.

A Financial System Without Borders

Bitcoin is financially based on principles that challenge the status quo: scarcity, decentralization, and trustless security. Its value is derived not only from its technological foundation but also from its ability to provide a global, inclusive, and inflation-resistant alternative to traditional money.

In a world where trust in institutions is waning, Bitcoin offers a new way forward—a financial system that is fairer, more transparent, and firmly in the hands of the people.

Part 3. Bitcoin in the Real World

Bitcoin's Journey Through the Decade: Milestones in Bitcoin's Growth

Bitcoin's evolution over the past decade has been nothing short of extraordinary. From its humble beginnings as an obscure idea shared among cryptographers to becoming a globally recognized financial asset, Bitcoin has experienced a journey filled with triumphs, challenges, and pivotal milestones. This part explores the key moments that have defined Bitcoin's growth and solidified its place in the financial and technological landscape.

1. The Genesis Block (2009)

Bitcoin's journey began on January 3, 2009, with the mining of the Genesis Block by its mysterious creator, Satoshi Nakamoto. Embedded within this block was a message:
"The Times 03/Jan/2009 Chancellor on brink of second bailout for banks."

This statement not only served as a timestamp but also a critique of the centralized financial system that Bitcoin sought to challenge. The Genesis Block marked the birth of a decentralized monetary system and laid the foundation for what would evolve into a global phenomenon.

2. The First Bitcoin Transaction (2009)

Shortly after Bitcoin's creation, Satoshi Nakamoto sent 10 BTC to Hal Finney, a cryptographer and early Bitcoin enthusiast. That marked the first-ever Bitcoin transaction and demonstrated the functionality of the peer-to-peer electronic cash system.

3. Bitcoin Pizza Day (2010)

On May 22, 2010, Bitcoin was used for the first time to purchase a real-world item. Laszlo Hanyecz, a programmer, paid 10,000 BTC for two pizzas—a transaction now worth hundreds of millions of dollars. This event, now celebrated annually as Bitcoin Pizza Day, demonstrated Bitcoin's utility as a medium of exchange and marked its first step toward mainstream adoption.

4. The Mt. Gox Era and the First Major Exchange (2010-2014)

Bitcoin's growth accelerated with the creation of Mt. Gox, one of the first Bitcoin exchanges. Launched in 2010, Mt. Gox allowed users to trade Bitcoin for fiat currency, making it easier for people to access and use the digital asset.

Growth and Collapse:
- At its peak, Mt. Gox handled over 70% of all Bitcoin transactions worldwide, becoming a cornerstone of the ecosystem.
- However, in 2014, the exchange was hacked, leading to the loss of 850,000 BTC (worth over $450 million at the time). The collapse shook confidence in Bitcoin and highlighted the need for more secure infrastructure.

5. The First Bitcoin Bull Run (2013)

Bitcoin's price surpassed $1,000 for the first time in late 2013, fueled by growing interest from tech enthusiasts and early adopters. This milestone drew significant attention to Bitcoin but also attracted increased regulatory scrutiny, especially in China, where exchanges were temporarily forced to halt operations.

6. Institutional Recognition Begins (2017)

The year 2017 was a watershed moment for Bitcoin:

- Bitcoin's Price Boom:
  Bitcoin's price skyrocketed from under $1,000 at the beginning of the year to nearly $20,000 by December, driven by retail investor enthusiasm and global media coverage.

- Scaling Challenges:
  The surge in adoption exposed Bitcoin's limitations, such as high transaction fees and slow processing times. This sparked debates about scaling solutions, ultimately leading to the implementation of Segregated Witness (SegWit) to enhance transaction efficiency. It is a change in the way transactions were signed by the nodes that act as witnesses on the Bitcoin blockchain.

- CME and CBOE Futures:
  CME (Chicago Mercantile Exchange) and CBOE (Chicago Board Options Exchange) are two of the largest financial exchanges in the world, each serving different roles in the trading and derivatives markets. The launch of Bitcoin futures trading on major exchanges like CME and CBOE marked a significant step toward institutional acceptance, allowing traditional investors to gain exposure to Bitcoin.

7. The Rise of Institutional Adoption (2020-2021)

Bitcoin entered a new era during the global COVID-19 pandemic, as economic uncertainty drove interest in alternative assets:

- Corporate Investments:
  - Companies like MicroStrategy, Tesla, and Square began adding Bitcoin to their balance sheets, citing it as a hedge against inflation.
  - MicroStrategy CEO Michael Saylor emerged as one of Bitcoin's most vocal proponents, investing billions into the digital asset.

- All-Time Highs:
  In 2021, Bitcoin reached an all-time high of $69,000, fueled by institutional demand and growing acceptance as a store of value.

- El Salvador Makes Bitcoin Legal Tender:
  In a historic move, El Salvador became the first country to adopt Bitcoin as legal tender in 2021, integrating it into its economy and paving the way for broader adoption by nations.

8. Regulatory Milestones and ETF Approvals (2021-2023)

As Bitcoin matured, regulatory clarity and the launch of new financial products further legitimized it:

- Bitcoin ETFs:
  The approval of Bitcoin-linked Exchange-Traded Funds (ETFs) in countries like the U.S. and Canada allowed investors to access Bitcoin through traditional investment vehicles.

  These ETFs, such as the ProShares Bitcoin Strategy ETF, attracted billions of dollars in investments, signaling mainstream acceptance.

- Global Regulation:
  Governments worldwide began formalizing their stances on Bitcoin, with some embracing it (e.g., Switzerland and the UAE) while others imposed restrictions (e.g., China's mining ban).

9. The Resilience of Bitcoin (2024 and Beyond)

Bitcoin's ability to recover from setbacks and continue growing underscores its resilience:

- Adoption in Emerging Markets:
  Bitcoin has become a lifeline in countries facing hyperinflation and economic instability, such as Venezuela, Nigeria, and Argentina.

- Technological Innovations:
  Developments like the Lightning Network have made Bitcoin transactions faster and cheaper, enhancing its utility as a medium of exchange.

- Long-Term Institutional Trust:
  As of 2024, major financial institutions, including BlackRock, have recognized Bitcoin as a legitimate asset class, further solidifying its place in the global economy.

A Decade of Transformation

In little more than a decade, Bitcoin has evolved from an obscure digital experiment to a multi-trillion-dollar asset class. Its milestones reflect a journey of resilience, innovation, and growing acceptance. While challenges remain, Bitcoin's impact on the world's financial and technological systems is undeniable, and its journey is far from over.

The Rise of Institutional Adoption and ETF Approvals

Bitcoin's journey toward mainstream acceptance reached a pivotal moment with the rise of institutional adoption and the approval of Bitcoin Exchange-Traded Funds (ETFs). These developments marked a significant shift, moving Bitcoin from a niche investment for early adopters to a recognized asset class embraced by some of the world's largest financial institutions.

The Rise of Institutional Adoption

Bitcoin spent much of its early history being disregarded by traditional financial institutions, often labeled as a speculative bubble or a haven for criminal activity. However, the narrative began to change dramatically in the late 2010s and early 2020s, as Bitcoin's resilience and potential as a store of value became harder to ignore.

Key Drivers of Institutional Interest

1. Inflation Hedging:
   The COVID-19 pandemic prompted central banks worldwide to engage in massive money printing, raising concerns about inflation and the devaluation of fiat currencies.

   Bitcoin, with its fixed supply of 21 million coins, emerged as a hedge against inflation and a viable alternative to gold.

2. Portfolio Diversification:
   Bitcoin's low correlation with traditional assets like stocks and bonds made it an attractive addition to institutional portfolios, providing potential returns while reducing overall risk.

3. Increased Liquidity:
   The rise of regulated Bitcoin exchanges and custodial services made it easier for institutions to buy, sell, and hold Bitcoin securely.

4. Endorsements from Financial Leaders:
   Prominent figures like Larry Fink, CEO of BlackRock, and Paul Tudor Jones, a legendary hedge fund manager, publicly expressed their belief in Bitcoin's potential. Fink referred to Bitcoin as an 'alternative source for wealth holding,' while Jones described it as 'the fastest horse in the race' against inflation.

Examples of Institutional Adoption

- MicroStrategy:
  In 2020, the business intelligence firm MicroStrategy, led by CEO Michael Saylor, became one of the first publicly traded companies to add Bitcoin to its balance sheet. As of 2024, the company holds over 150,000 BTC.

- Tesla:
  In early 2021, Tesla announced a $1.5 billion Bitcoin investment, further validating its role as a corporate treasury asset.

- BlackRock and Fidelity:
  BlackRock, the world's largest asset manager, and Fidelity both launched crypto investment products, signaling the entry of traditional finance into the Bitcoin ecosystem.

- Banks and Payment Giants:
  Companies like PayPal, Square (now Block), and Visa integrated Bitcoin into their platforms, enabling millions of users to buy, sell, and transact with Bitcoin seamlessly.

ETF Approvals: Bridging Traditional and Crypto Markets

What is a Bitcoin ETF?

A Bitcoin ETF (Exchange-Traded Fund) is a financial product that tracks the price of Bitcoin and trades on traditional stock exchanges. It allows investors to gain exposure to Bitcoin without dealing with the complexities of managing private keys, wallets, or exchanges.

The approval of Bitcoin ETFs was a watershed moment, making it easier for retail and institutional investors to gain exposure to Bitcoin through familiar financial products. ETFs allow investors to buy shares that track Bitcoin's price without the need to directly hold or manage the cryptocurrency.

The Journey to ETF Approvals

The road to Bitcoin ETF approval was long and fraught with challenges. For years, regulators like the U.S. Securities and Exchange Commission (SEC) rejected applications, citing concerns over market manipulation, volatility, and a lack of investor protections.

Key Milestones in ETF Approvals

Canada Leads the Way (2021)

Canada became the first country to approve Bitcoin ETFs in February 2021. The Purpose Bitcoin ETF (BTCC) launched on the Toronto Stock Exchange and quickly attracted over $1 billion in assets. This approval paved the way for other countries to explore similar products.

ProShares Bitcoin Strategy ETF (2021)

In October 2021, the U.S. Securities and Exchange Commission (SEC) approved the ProShares Bitcoin Strategy ETF (BITO), making it the first Bitcoin-linked ETF in the United States.

Unlike spot ETFs, which physically hold Bitcoin, this ETF derives its value from Bitcoin futures contracts. Despite this limitation, it was seen as a major step toward mainstream adoption and generated significant interest, with over $1 billion in trading volume in its first two days.

The Approval of Spot Bitcoin ETFs in the U.S.: A Turning Point in Cryptocurrency Adoption

In January 2024, the U.S. Securities and Exchange Commission (SEC) made a groundbreaking decision, approving the first-ever spot Bitcoin exchange-traded funds (ETFs). This long-awaited milestone opened the doors for institutional investors and individuals to gain direct exposure to Bitcoin through regulated financial products, marking a significant leap in the mainstream adoption of cryptocurrencies. Spot Bitcoin ETFs are now accessible, allowing investors to gain exposure to Bitcoin backed by actual cryptocurrency holdings, unlike futures-based ETFs.

The introduction of spot Bitcoin ETFs allowed asset management giants, including BlackRock, Fidelity, Grayscale, and ARK Invest, to launch innovative investment vehicles. These funds enable investors to participate in the Bitcoin market without the challenges of directly managing and securing the cryptocurrency themselves.

The market response to this approval was monumental. Bitcoin experienced an unprecedented surge, with its price soaring to an all-time high above $100,000 by the end of 2024. This rapid growth was fueled by increased confidence in Bitcoin as a credible and institutional-grade asset, bolstered by the regulated nature of these ETFs.

BlackRock's iShares Bitcoin Trust emerged as a standout performer, attracting over $53 billion in assets within its first eleven months. Other notable funds, such as Fidelity's Wise Origin Bitcoin Fund and Grayscale's Bitcoin Trust ETF, also drew significant investor interest, further solidifying Bitcoin's status as a key asset in modern investment portfolios. Since their introduction, they have attracted more than $100 billion in investments, breaking records and cementing Bitcoin's place in the mainstream financial ecosystem. As of the writing of this book, Bitcoin ETFs are the most successful ETFs in Wall Street history, reflecting their immense appeal to retail and institutional investors.

The SEC's approval came after years of scrutiny and rejections of similar proposals, primarily due to concerns over market manipulation and investor safety. However, the decision in 2024 reflected the evolution of the regulatory landscape and the growing demand for legitimate, well-structured Bitcoin investment options.

This regulatory milestone not only elevated Bitcoin but also set the stage for additional cryptocurrency-based ETFs, including those tied to Ethereum. The approval underscored a broader shift towards recognizing digital assets as an integral part of the financial ecosystem.

The acceptance of spot Bitcoin ETFs represents a pivotal chapter in Bitcoin's journey. It signals a growing integration of cryptocurrencies into traditional markets, providing investors with new opportunities while reshaping the perception of digital assets in the global economy.

Impact of ETF Approvals

1. Accessibility for Retail Investors:
    ETFs make Bitcoin accessible to a broader audience, including traditional investors who may not be comfortable navigating cryptocurrency exchanges or managing wallets. They enable Bitcoin to be incorporated into retirement accounts and investment portfolios without facing regulatory barriers.

2. Legitimization of Bitcoin:
    ETF approvals signal a growing acceptance of Bitcoin as a legitimate financial asset. That increases confidence among hesitant investors and reinforces Bitcoin's place in mainstream finance.

3. Institutional Inflows:
    The availability of ETFs has facilitated billions of dollars in institutional inflows, further stabilizing Bitcoin's market and increasing liquidity.

4. Global Trends:
    Countries like Australia, Brazil, and Germany have followed Canada's lead, approving Bitcoin ETFs and reflecting a global trend toward greater regulatory acceptance.

The Future of Bitcoin ETFs

The push for spot Bitcoin ETFs is expected to dominate the next phase of Bitcoin's institutional adoption:

- Spot ETFs, which directly hold Bitcoin, are seen as the next step in bringing genuine price exposure and transparency to the market.
- Approval of these products could unlock trillions of dollars in potential investments from institutional players like pension funds, mutual funds, and sovereign wealth funds.

The rise of institutional adoption and ETF approvals has transformed Bitcoin from a niche digital currency to a globally recognized financial asset. These milestones have bridged the gap between traditional and crypto markets, enabling investors of all types to participate in Bitcoin's growth story. With institutions like BlackRock and Grayscale leading the charge, Bitcoin's integration into the global financial system is accelerating, paving the way for even greater adoption in the years to come.

How Bitcoin ETFs Work

Bitcoin ETFs provide a way for investors to gain exposure to Bitcoin without having to buy or manage the cryptocurrency directly. Here's how they work and who they're designed for:

1. What Does a Bitcoin ETF Do?

A Bitcoin ETF tracks the price of Bitcoin, allowing investors to buy shares in the ETF that mirror Bitcoin's market performance. When Bitcoin's price rises, the value of the ETF rises correspondingly, and vice versa. ETFs can be based on:

- Futures Contracts: These ETFs invest in Bitcoin futures rather than holding Bitcoin directly. For example, the ProShares Bitcoin Strategy ETF (BITO) operates on Bitcoin futures contracts.
- Spot ETFs: These ETFs hold actual Bitcoin in custody.

2. Who Are Bitcoin ETFs Designed For?

Bitcoin ETFs are primarily aimed at:

- Institutional Investors and Corporations:
  Large institutions, pension funds, and corporations often prefer ETFs because they fit seamlessly into traditional financial systems.

  ETFs are regulated, making them more palatable for entities bound by strict compliance requirements.

- Governments:
  Sovereign wealth funds or state-backed institutions may use ETFs to gain Bitcoin exposure without directly managing private keys.

- Retail Investors Unfamiliar with Crypto Custody:
  Individuals hesitant to handle private keys or use cryptocurrency exchanges may find ETFs an easier entry point into Bitcoin investment.

The Custody Question: Who Owns Bitcoin in ETFs?

One of the most important aspects of Bitcoin ETFs is understanding custody and ownership:

1. Custody by ETF Issuers:

   - When you invest in a Bitcoin ETF, you don't actually own Bitcoin.
   - The Bitcoin is held by the ETF issuer or its custodian, such as BlackRock or Grayscale. The issuer manages the Bitcoin on behalf of the ETF and ensures it's secure.

2. Limitations of Bitcoin ETFs:
   - No Ownership: ETF investors own shares in the fund, not the Bitcoin itself.
     That means:
       - You can't transfer Bitcoin from an ETF to your wallet.
       - You can't use Bitcoin for payments or generate yield through DeFi or staking.
   - Lack of Freedom: Bitcoin ETFs don't offer the financial sovereignty that Bitcoin was designed for, as outlined in the original whitepaper.

3. For True Bitcoin Ownership:
   - If you want to experience the freedom of money and value that Bitcoin promises, you need to own Bitcoin directly, not through an ETF.
   - Direct ownership allows you to:
       - Transfer Bitcoin anywhere in the world without restrictions.
       - Custody your Bitcoin securely using wallets (explained later in this book).
       - Fully control your wealth without relying on third-party institutions.

Bitcoin ETFs vs. Owning Bitcoin

Aspect	Bitcoin ETF	Owning Bitcoin Directly
Ownership	No actual Bitcoin ownership	You own the Bitcoin
Transferability	Cannot be transferred or used as a payment	Fully transferable globally
Custody	Held by ETF issuer or custodian	You hold it yourself (or choose a custodian)
Yield Generation	No yield options	Can generate yield through DeFi or staking

Bitcoin ETFs and the Individuals

While Bitcoin ETFs are excellent for institutions and individuals who seek a simple investment vehicle, they miss the essence of Bitcoin's original mission: financial sovereignty and freedom. Bitcoin was designed to put the power of money back into the hands of individuals, removing the need for intermediaries. ETFs, by design, reintroduce intermediaries.

For the ordinary individual who values the freedom of money, buying Bitcoin is the way to go.

That involves:

1. Purchasing Bitcoin from a reputable exchange.

2. Safely custodying your Bitcoin using wallets (which we'll explain later in this book).

3. Taking control of your financial future without reliance on third-party custodians.

Bitcoin ETFs—A Step Forward, But Not the Final Destination

Bitcoin ETFs represent a significant milestone in the journey of Bitcoin's adoption. They have opened the doors for institutional investors, provided legitimacy to Bitcoin as an asset class, and made Bitcoin more accessible to traditional investors.

However, they are not without limitations. ETFs offer exposure to Bitcoin's price, but they do not capture its core values of freedom, sovereignty, and decentralization. For those who want to fully embrace Bitcoin's potential, owning and self-custodying Bitcoin is the real way to experience the financial revolution it offers.

In the next parts, we'll cover how to securely buy and store Bitcoin, empowering you to fully own your digital wealth.

Statements from Financial Leaders

Larry Fink (CEO of BlackRock) on Bitcoin and Its Role in Digital Finance

As the CEO of BlackRock, the world's largest asset manager with over $10 trillion in assets under management, Larry Fink holds a significant sway in the global financial landscape. His evolving stance on Bitcoin reflects the broader journey of institutional finance toward embracing digital assets. From skepticism to advocacy, Fink's public statements have played a crucial role in shaping Bitcoin's position in digital finance.

The Evolution of Larry Fink's Perspective

Larry Fink's views on Bitcoin have shifted dramatically over the years:

1. Initial Skepticism:
    - Like many traditional finance leaders, Fink was initially cautious about Bitcoin. In its early days, Bitcoin was often dismissed as a speculative asset with minimal inherent value.
    - Fink expressed concerns about Bitcoin's volatility and its association with illegal activities, reflecting the sentiment of much of Wall Street at the time.
2. The Turning Point:
    - By 2023, Fink's tone had shifted. Recognizing the growing demand for digital assets among institutional and retail investors, he acknowledged Bitcoin's potential as a legitimate financial asset.
    - This change coincided with BlackRock's application for a spot Bitcoin ETF, signaling the firm's commitment to integrating Bitcoin into traditional financial systems.
3. Embracing Bitcoin's Role in Digital Finance:
    - In 2024, Fink declared himself a 'big believer' in Bitcoin. He publicly described it as a 'global asset' and a potential 'alternative source for wealth holding.'
    - He emphasized Bitcoin's utility as a digital gold, likening its role in modern finance to that of precious metals in the past.

Notable Statements by Larry Fink

1. On Bitcoin as an Alternative Wealth Store:

   "I'm a big believer in Bitcoin because I do believe it is an alternative source for wealth holding."

   Fink highlighted Bitcoin's appeal in a world where fiat currencies are increasingly questioned, particularly due to inflation and central bank policies.

2. On Bitcoin's Global Role:

   "If you're in a country where you're fearful of your future, fearful of your government, or you're frightened that your government is devaluing its currency by too much deficits, you can say this is a great potential long-term store of value. Like I said, it's like digital gold."

   This statement highlighted Bitcoin's growing importance in emerging markets and unstable economies, where it provides financial independence and protection from currency devaluation.

3. On Bitcoin as a Hedge Against Inflation:

   Fink has spoken about Bitcoin's role as a hedge against inflation, particularly in a post-pandemic world marked by massive government spending and monetary stimulus.

4. On Institutional Adoption:

   "Bitcoin's integration into traditional finance is inevitable. The more transparency and regulation we have, the more trust we can build, and the bigger the opportunities become."

   Fink's advocacy for regulatory clarity aligns with BlackRock's push for a regulated spot Bitcoin ETF, which has already seen success.

BlackRock's Impact on Bitcoin

Under Fink's leadership, BlackRock has played a pivotal role in legitimizing Bitcoin:

- Spot Bitcoin ETF: BlackRock's application for a spot Bitcoin ETF was a landmark moment, signaling that the world's largest asset manager viewed Bitcoin as a credible investment.
- Bitcoin Custody: BlackRock's custodial services for Bitcoin have further bridged the gap between traditional and digital finance.
- Institutional Influence: With its immense resources and credibility, BlackRock's embrace of Bitcoin has encouraged other financial institutions to follow suit.

Larry Fink's Legacy in Digital Finance

Fink's recognition of Bitcoin's potential is more than just a personal belief—it reflects the shifting mindset of institutional finance. By comparing Bitcoin to digital gold and championing its role in wealth preservation, Fink has positioned BlackRock at the forefront of the digital finance revolution.

His leadership demonstrates that Bitcoin is no longer just a speculative asset; it is a global financial instrument with the power to reshape how value is stored, transferred, and secured. Fink's statements and actions have not only legitimized Bitcoin in the eyes of skeptics but also paved the way for its adoption on an unprecedented scale.

Michael Saylor: The Bitcoin Evangelist and His Success Story

As of November 27, 2024, Michael Saylor remains one of the most influential and vocal advocates of Bitcoin. Known as the Bitcoin evangelist, Saylor has transformed his company, MicroStrategy, and his wealth by embracing Bitcoin as a cornerstone of financial strategy. His bold moves and articulate defense of Bitcoin have earned him a legendary status in the crypto community and beyond.

Michael Saylor's Success with Bitcoin

The MicroStrategy Revolution

Michael Saylor is the co-founder and Executive Chairman of MicroStrategy, a business intelligence firm that was once relatively unknown outside of tech circles. That changed dramatically in August 2020, when Saylor announced that MicroStrategy had adopted Bitcoin as its primary treasury reserve asset.

1. Initial Investment:
   - MicroStrategy purchased 21,454 BTC for $250 million at an average price of about $11,650 per Bitcoin.
   - Saylor described this move as a hedge against inflation, expressing concerns about the U.S. dollar's weakening purchasing power due to excessive money printing.
2. Ongoing Accumulation:
   - MicroStrategy continued buying Bitcoin aggressively, using corporate cash, proceeds from stock offerings, and even convertible debt to fund purchases.
   - As of November 2024, MicroStrategy holds over 386,700 BTC, acquired at an average price of approximately $56,761 per Bitcoin.
   - This investment, now worth over $38 billion (at the moment of this book written), has solidified MicroStrategy as one of the largest Bitcoin holders in the world and catapulted the company's market capitalization.
   - Saylor Plans to Raise $42B to Buy More Bitcoin Over Next 3 Years.
3. Shareholder Rewards:
   - The Bitcoin strategy significantly boosted MicroStrategy's stock price, attracting new investors and increasing shareholder value.
   - Saylor often describes MicroStrategy as a business intelligence company and a Bitcoin proxy, giving investors indirect exposure to Bitcoin through the stock.

Personal Success

Saylor has also become one of the wealthiest Bitcoin holders.

Reports suggest that he owns over 17,000 BTC purchased at an average price of $9,800. These holdings alone have made him a billionaire several times over.

His advocacy has transcended his corporate role, as he dedicates significant time and resources to educating people about Bitcoin through public speaking, interviews, and social media.

Michael Saylor's Most Notable Statements on Bitcoin

On Bitcoin's Superiority Over Gold:

"Bitcoin is digital gold. It's harder, smarter, faster, and stronger than any money that has preceded it."

Saylor frequently emphasizes Bitcoin's superiority to gold as a store of value due to its portability, verifiability, and scarcity.

On Inflation and Fiat Currency:

"The U.S. dollar is a melting ice cube. Every fiat currency in the world is devaluing as central banks print trillions of dollars. Bitcoin is the solution."

This analogy of a 'melting ice cube' has become iconic, encapsulating Saylor's belief that fiat currencies erode wealth over time due to inflation.

On Bitcoin as the Ultimate Asset:

"There's no property in the world better than Bitcoin. Not stocks, not bonds, not gold, not real estate. Nothing."

Saylor argues that Bitcoin is the ultimate asset class because it combines scarcity, security, and global accessibility.

On Bitcoin's Adoption Curve:

"We're still in the early innings. Bitcoin is going to go from 1% of the world owning it to 5%, then 50%. It's just a matter of time."

This reflects his belief in Bitcoin's massive potential for global adoption, driven by increasing awareness and utility.

On Bitcoin's Role in Technology:

"Bitcoin is the most important technology of the 21st century. It's a monetary network that will last forever."

Saylor views Bitcoin not just as a financial asset but as a transformative innovation on par with the internet.

On Holding Bitcoin:

"If you understand Bitcoin, you buy it. If you don't understand Bitcoin, you sell it. If you really understand Bitcoin, you HODL it."

Saylor champions a long-term investment strategy, dismissing short-term trading in favor of holding Bitcoin through market volatility.

On Bitcoin's Price Potential:

"Bitcoin will hit $1 million per coin. It's not a matter of if, but when."

Saylor's price predictions are bold but grounded in Bitcoin's fixed supply and increasing demand from institutional investors.

The Legacy of Michael Saylor

Michael Saylor's unwavering belief in Bitcoin has reshaped his company, his personal brand, and the perception of Bitcoin in the institutional finance world. He has:

- Positioned MicroStrategy as a leader in Bitcoin adoption.

- Inspired countless corporations and institutional investors to consider Bitcoin as a treasury asset.

- Become one of the most recognized voices in the crypto space, dedicating his resources to promoting Bitcoin education and adoption.

A Visionary Advocate

Saylor's advocacy goes beyond profit. He sees Bitcoin as a tool for economic empowerment, financial freedom, and innovation. His relentless optimism and articulate defense of Bitcoin have made him a trusted figure in the crypto community and a respected leader in the financial world.

Part 4. Bitcoin as Digital Gold

Introduction

In the vast, digital expanse of the 21st century, a new asset class has emerged, promising to redefine wealth in a manner reminiscent of gold's storied history. This asset is Bitcoin, often heralded as 'digital gold.' But what does it mean to call Bitcoin digital gold, and why has this analogy become so pervasive in financial discussions? Let's delve into this fascinating comparison.

The Genesis of Gold

Gold has been revered across civilizations for its luster, scarcity, and durability. For millennia, it served as a store of value, a medium of exchange, and a symbol of wealth. Its intrinsic qualities made it a natural choice for currency, jewelry, and, later, reserve assets in national treasuries.

- Scarcity: The total amount of gold ever mined would fit into just two Olympic swimming pools, making it rare enough to maintain its value over time.

- Universal Appeal: Across cultures and epochs, gold has been a constant measure of wealth, trusted for its stability and intrinsic worth.

Bitcoin: The Digital Counterpart

Bitcoin, created in 2009 by the pseudonymous Satoshi Nakamoto, was introduced as a response to the failures of the traditional financial system exposed during the 2008 financial crisis. Here is where the comparison to gold begins:

1. Scarcity: Bitcoin's supply is capped at 21 million coins, a limit coded into its protocol. This scarcity is immutable and predictable, making it analogous to the physical rarity of gold. Unlike fiat currencies, Bitcoin's supply cannot be manipulated by governments or central banks.

2. Decentralization: Just as gold is not controlled by any single entity, Bitcoin operates on a decentralized network of computers, ensuring that no government or institution can seize control of its issuance or policies.
3. Durability and Portability:
   - Gold is durable but cumbersome to transport.
   - Bitcoin is infinitely portable, divisible, and easy to store. It can be transferred across the globe in seconds, offering advantages gold cannot match.
4. Store of Value:
   - Both gold and Bitcoin have long been considered safe havens in times of economic turmoil.
   - Bitcoin adds modern attributes to this role, such as resistance to censorship and seizure, making it even more appealing in uncertain times.

The journey of Bitcoin as digital gold is still unfolding. While it shares many fundamental characteristics with physical gold—scarcity, durability, and a role as a store of value—Bitcoin introduces revolutionary features like divisibility, instant transferability, and full transparency through blockchain technology.

Like gold, Bitcoin offers a hedge against inflation and economic uncertainty, but it also introduces modern advantages tailored to the digital age. Let's analyze its use case as a store of value in detail.

The Concept of a Store of Value

A store of value is any asset that can:

- Retain its purchasing power over time.
- Protect against economic and monetary instability.
- Serve as a reliable reservoir of wealth.

For centuries, gold has been the benchmark store of value due to its scarcity, durability, and independence from any single government or institution. In the modern era, Bitcoin has emerged as a digital counterpart to gold, with its unique advantages.

Bitcoin vs. Traditional Stores of Value

Attribute	Gold	Real Estate	Bitcoin
Scarcity	Limited but not capped	Finite but not portable	Hard cap of 21 million coins
Portability	Heavy, costly to transport	Immobile	Easily transferable worldwide
Divisibility	Limited (to small units)	Not divisible	Divisible into 100 million satoshis
Liquidity	Moderate	Low	High, 24/7 markets worldwide
Censorship Resistance	Moderate	Low	High

Bitcoin vs. Stocks

Aspect	Bitcoin	Stocks
Ownership	Decentralized, no controlling entity	Tied to a single company, influenced by management
Market Hours	Trades 24/7 worldwide	Limited to exchange hours
Volatility	Highly volatile	Moderate volatility
Yield	No dividends or yields	Dividends and potential capital appreciation

Historical Performance as a Store of Value

Bitcoin's price history highlights its growing appeal as a store of value:

1. Exponential Growth:
   In its first decade, Bitcoin's value surged from less than $0.01 to an all-time high of nearly $69,000 in 2021. This extraordinary growth reflects increasing demand and limited supply.

   Bitcoin's adoption curve mirrors transformative technologies like the internet, suggesting further upside potential.

2. Volatility:
   While Bitcoin's volatility has been a concern, its long-term trajectory has been overwhelmingly positive. Over time, as adoption increases and liquidity grows, volatility is expected to decrease.

3. Market Events:
   - 2017 Bull Run: Bitcoin's price skyrocketed to $20,000, fueled by retail investor interest.

   - 2020-2021 Pandemic Era: Bitcoin reached $69,000 as institutional adoption soared during economic uncertainty.

   - 2024 ETF Approvals: Spot Bitcoin ETFs brought billions in institutional investments, further stabilizing Bitcoin's market.

   - 2024 (By the time this book was written) Bitcoin has already surpassed $104,000.

Conclusion

One of Bitcoin's most compelling attributes is its use case as a store of value. Combining scarcity, portability, and resistance to censorship, it provides a modern alternative to traditional stores of value like gold and real estate. While challenges remain, Bitcoin's adoption trajectory suggests that it will continue to redefine how individuals, institutions, and even nations preserve wealth in the digital age.

Historical Price Trends and Patterns of Bitcoin

Bitcoin's price history is a captivating tale of rapid growth, extreme volatility, and remarkable resilience. Its journey from a niche experiment to a multi-trillion-dollar asset class offers insights into its unique nature as a digital asset and its potential for long-term value appreciation. Let's dive into the key historical price trends and patterns that have defined Bitcoin's evolution.

1. Early Days: Bitcoin's Infancy (2009-2012)

- 2009:
  At its inception, Bitcoin had no monetary value. It was traded only among early adopters and enthusiasts who saw it as an innovative experiment.

- 2010 – First Real-World Transaction:
  On May 22, 2010, Laszlo Hanyecz famously purchased two pizzas for 10,000 BTC, marking the first real-world transaction using Bitcoin. That valued Bitcoin at $0.004 per coin.

- 2011 – Reaching $1:
  Bitcoin hit $1 for the first time in February 2011, attracting attention from the broader tech community. Later that year, Bitcoin's price spiked to $31, only to crash back to $2 after speculation-driven hype faded.

2. The First Bull Run: Crossing $1,000 (2013)

- 2013 – Early Institutional Interest:
  Bitcoin saw its first major bull run, rising from $13 in January to over $1,000 in November.

  The price surge was driven by:

  - Increased adoption by early exchanges like Mt. Gox.

  - Growing awareness among tech-savvy individuals.

  - Speculative trading.

- Crash to $200:
  After peaking at $1,000, Bitcoin's price collapsed due to regulatory scrutiny and the Mt. Gox hack, which shook confidence in the ecosystem.

3. Consolidation Period: Stability Before the Storm (2014-2016)

During this period, Bitcoin traded between $200 and $600, with slower adoption and reduced media attention.

Key events during this time:

- 2014 – Mt. Gox Collapse: The loss of 850,000 BTC undermined trust in the ecosystem and spurred advancements in security and infrastructure.

- 2015 – Lightning Network Announced: This innovation promised to address Bitcoin's scalability issues, boosting optimism about its long-term viability.

4. The 2017 Bull Run: Breaking $20,000

- Exponential Growth:

  Bitcoin's price skyrocketed from $1,000 in January 2017 to nearly $20,000 by December 2017, marking its most famous bull run.

  Drivers included:

  - Increased media coverage.

  - The rise of Initial Coin Offerings (ICOs), which fueled speculative investments. Initial Coin Offerings are events in which a company sells a new cryptocurrency to raise funds.

  - Greater global interest, particularly in Asia.

- The Crash:

  By early 2018, Bitcoin's price dropped by over 80%, falling to $3,200 by December. That marked the start of a bear market, often called the 'crypto winter.'

5. The Institutional Era: COVID-19 Pandemic and Beyond (2020-2024)

- 2020 – The COVID-19 Effect:
    - Bitcoin rebounded as the COVID-19 pandemic highlighted the risks of fiat currency inflation due to massive government stimulus packages.
    - Institutional investors, including MicroStrategy, Tesla, and hedge funds, began adopting Bitcoin as a treasury reserve asset.
    - Bitcoin crossed $20,000 in December 2020, hitting an all-time high and entering mainstream financial discussions.
- 2021 – $69,000 All-Time High:
    - Bitcoin reached $64,000 in April 2021, fueled by:
        - Retail adoption through platforms like PayPal.
        - El Salvador adopting Bitcoin as legal tender.
        - Increased institutional buying.
    - After a mid-year correction, Bitcoin surged again to hit its all-time high of $69,000 in November 2021, driven by:
        - Anticipation of regulatory clarity.
        - The launch of the first Bitcoin futures ETFs in the U.S.
- 2022 – Bear Market:
    - The collapse of major crypto firms like Terra (LUNA) and FTX triggered a sharp market downturn. Bitcoin's price fell below $20,000, shaking confidence in the broader crypto market.
- 2024 – Recovery and ETF Approvals:
    - Bitcoin rebounded as the U.S. approved several spot Bitcoin ETFs, signaling increased institutional acceptance.
    - BlackRock and Grayscale became major players, driving Bitcoin's price back above $50,000, as investors viewed ETFs as a secure entry point into the market.
    - After Trump's Victory in the US Election, Bitcoin reached a new all-time high, surpassing $103,000.

6. Patterns in Bitcoin's Price History

1. Halving Cycles

   Bitcoin undergoes a halving event approximately every four years, reducing the mining reward by half. This event significantly impacts supply and often precedes major bull runs.

   Past halvings and reductions in mining rewards resulted in:
   - 2012: Price increased from $12 to $260.
   - 2016: Price rose from $650 to $20,000.
   - 2020: Price surged from $8,500 to $69,000 by late 2021.
   - The next halving in 2024 is expected to catalyze another bull market.
   - In December 2024 Bitcoin Reached a new all-time high of $103,000.

2. Boom and Bust Cycles

   Bitcoin's price history follows a recurring pattern:

   - Bull Markets: Periods of rapid growth driven by adoption, speculation, or macroeconomic factors.
   - Bear Markets: Corrections that shake out speculative investments and pave the way for long-term growth.

3. Correlation with Macro Trends

   Bitcoin's price often correlates with global economic events:
   - Inflationary periods drive demand for Bitcoin as a hedge.
   - Market downturns can create selling pressure as investors seek liquidity.

7. Bitcoin's Resilience

Despite multiple crashes and periods of doubt, Bitcoin has consistently recovered and reached new highs. Its ability to withstand challenges like exchange hacks, regulatory scrutiny, and market manipulation underscores its strength as a revolutionary financial asset.

Conclusion: A Roadmap to the Future

Bitcoin's historical price trends and patterns reveal a story of resilience, growth, and increasing adoption. While its volatility can be intimidating, the long-term trajectory suggests an upward trend driven by scarcity, utility, and growing institutional support. Understanding these patterns is crucial for appreciating Bitcoin's potential as a store of value and a transformative force in global finance.

Part 5. Institutional and Government Adoption of Bitcoin

Bitcoin's journey from a niche digital currency to a globally recognized asset has been significantly bolstered by institutional and government adoption. While early adoption was led by tech enthusiasts and retail investors, the involvement of countries, banks, and institutional investors has elevated Bitcoin to a legitimate asset class with significant implications for global finance.

Countries Adopting Bitcoin as a Legal Tender

El Salvador: The Pioneer

In September 2021, El Salvador became the first country in the world to adopt Bitcoin as legal tender. This groundbreaking move, spearheaded by President Nayib Bukele, was designed to:

- Promote Financial Inclusion: Approximately 70% of El Salvador's population lacked access to traditional banking services. Bitcoin provided a means for unbanked citizens to participate in the economy.
- Attract Investment: The government aimed to position El Salvador as a hub for crypto innovation, attracting investors and companies in the blockchain space.
- Reduce Remittance Costs: A significant portion of El Salvador's GDP comes from remittances sent by citizens abroad. Bitcoin enabled cheaper and faster cross-border transactions.

Bitcoin Strategic Reserve

U.S. Government Bitcoin Strategic Reserve

The U.S. Government Bitcoin Strategic Reserve has been a topic of significant discussion, especially in light of Donald Trump's recent election and his campaign promises concerning cryptocurrency.

Legislation and Plans

Senator Cynthia Lummis introduced the 'BITCOIN Act of 2024,' which proposes a strategic Bitcoin reserve establishment by having the U.S. Treasury acquire 1 million BTC over five years, with an annual purchase of 200,000 BTC. This would be approximately 5% of the total Bitcoin supply, akin to the U.S.'s gold reserves.

The plan involves establishing a decentralized network of secure Bitcoin vaults managed by the U.S. Department of the Treasury, with strict rules on holding and selling, aimed at using Bitcoin as a hedge against inflation and potentially managing national debt.

President-elect Donald Trump has endorsed the idea of a Bitcoin reserve, suggesting it could help address the national debt, which exceeds $35 trillion. He has pledged not to sell existing Bitcoin holdings and to create a national stockpile.

Legislative Proposals

There have been discussions in the U.S. and now even state-level initiatives (like Pennsylvania's recent bill) about potentially holding Bitcoin in strategic reserves, akin to how nations hold gold or foreign currencies.

Economic Sovereignty

For some nations, Bitcoin represents an opportunity to assert economic sovereignty in a globalized world where traditional financial systems are frequently dominated by a few powerful currencies.

Russia's Bitcoin Strategic Reserve
Proposal

In the Russian State Duma (one of the two houses of the parliament of Russia), the Deputy Anton Tkachev of the New People party has proposed establishing a Bitcoin reserve for Russia. This proposal aims to complement traditional currency reserves with Bitcoin, viewing it as a hedge against economic sanctions, inflation, and currency volatility.

Motivation

The initiative stems from geopolitical tensions that have made traditional currencies like the dollar and euro less reliable for Russia. Bitcoin is viewed as an asset independent of any single nation's control, providing a potential buffer against financial isolation.

Current Status

While the proposal has been submitted to the Finance Minister for consideration, there's no indication yet of its approval or implementation. Russia has, however, taken steps to legalize and regulate cryptocurrency, including Bitcoin mining.

Global Context

This move aligns with a broader trend in which countries are considering Bitcoin reserves to diversify their financial assets, following examples such as El Salvador's adoption of Bitcoin as legal tender.

Japan's Bitcoin Strategic Reserve

Proposal

Japanese Senator Satoshi Hamada has advocated for a national Bitcoin reserve, arguing it could help address global economic challenges and protect national assets amid the Bitcoin's price surge.

Economic Rationale

Japan faces significant debt issues, with a debt-to-GDP ratio among the highest in the advanced economies. The idea is to use Bitcoin as a hedge against the depreciation of the yen and fiscal imprudence.

Implementation

There's no clear timeline or official endorsement yet. However, companies like Metaplanet in Japan have already begun adopting Bitcoin as a reserve asset, reflecting a growing acceptance of cryptocurrencies in the corporate world. Broader Implications: Japan's interest in Bitcoin reserves could signal a shift in how nations manage their economic stability, especially in an era where digital currencies gain legitimacy.

El Salvador's bold experiment inspired interest from other nations, particularly those with unstable currencies or heavy reliance on remittances:

- Central African Republic (CAR): In 2022, CAR became the second country to adopt Bitcoin as legal tender, citing goals of financial inclusion and modernization.
- Potential Candidates: Countries like Argentina, Turkey, and Venezuela have seen growing grassroots Bitcoin adoption due to hyperinflation and economic instability, though official legal tender status remains speculative.

Regulation and Control

Regulatory Frameworks

Many governments are developing or have established frameworks to regulate cryptocurrencies. The Markets of EU in Crypto-Assets (MiCA) regulation is one example, aiming to provide clarity and safety in the crypto space.

Taxation

Governments are eager to figure out how to tax Bitcoin transactions or holdings, a move that could lead to broader acceptance or stifle growth if perceived as overly punitive.

Institutional and government adoption of Bitcoin marks a significant evolution in the financial landscape. It is not just about speculative trading anymore; it is about recognizing Bitcoin's potential as a legitimate asset class and a tool for economic policy. This trend, while still in its nascent stages, could lead to profound changes in how we think about money, value storage, and global economic interactions. However, the path forward is fraught with challenges that must be navigated carefully to ensure this digital asset fulfills its promise without compromising financial stability or security.

Institutional Investors

The entry of institutional investors has solidified Bitcoin's reputation as a legitimate asset class: 60% of the largest Hedge Funds have disclosed #Bitcoin BTC ETF holdings.

Bitcoin as a Potential Reserve Currency?

The concept of Bitcoin as a global reserve currency challenges the traditional dominance of fiat currencies like the U.S. dollar. While still speculative, Bitcoin's attributes make it a compelling candidate for this role.

Why Bitcoin Could Become a Reserve Currency

1. Scarcity and Decentralization:
   - Unlike fiat currencies, which can be printed in unlimited quantities, Bitcoin's supply is capped at 21 million coins, ensuring long-term value retention.

   - Bitcoin's decentralized nature makes it immune to manipulation by any single government or central authority, offering a neutral and global alternative to national currencies.

2. Inflation Resistance:
   - As central banks worldwide grapple with inflation caused by excessive money printing, Bitcoin's deflationary properties make it an attractive alternative for countries looking to stabilize their reserves.

3. Borderless and Neutral:
   - Bitcoin is not tied to any nation-state, making it an appealing choice for countries wary of overreliance on the U.S. dollar or other dominant currencies.

Current Trends Toward Bitcoin as a Reserve Asset

1. Central Bank Experiments:
   - While no major central bank has officially adopted Bitcoin as a reserve currency, some are exploring it as a hedge:
     - Russia and Iran have discussed using Bitcoin for international trade to bypass sanctions.
     - Small island nations are considering Bitcoin to attract investment and diversify their economies.
2. Institutional Reserve Assets:
   - Institutions like Grayscale and BlackRock have indirectly positioned Bitcoin as a reserve-like asset, holding massive amounts on behalf of investors.
   - The approval of spot Bitcoin ETFs has made it easier for institutional investors to treat Bitcoin as a reserve asset within their portfolios.
3. Sovereign Wealth Funds:
   - Reports suggest that some sovereign wealth funds are beginning to allocate small percentages of their portfolios to Bitcoin, viewing it as a hedge against currency risk.

The adoption of Bitcoin by governments, banks, and institutions highlights its transition from a speculative asset to a legitimate financial instrument. While countries like El Salvador and corporations like MicroStrategy have demonstrated its use in treasury management, the broader question of Bitcoin's potential as a global reserve currency remains open. Its fixed supply, decentralization, and resistance to inflation make it an attractive candidate, but challenges like volatility and regulatory uncertainty must be addressed.

As adoption grows and the global financial system evolves, Bitcoin's role as a transformative force in institutional and government finance seems inevitable. Whether it becomes the world's reserve currency or remains a powerful store of value, its influence on the future of money is undeniable.

Part 6. The Investment Case for Bitcoin

Bitcoin has evolved from an obscure technological experiment to a cornerstone of modern financial discussions. Its emergence as a decentralized and scarce digital asset offers unprecedented opportunities for personal and institutional investors to protect wealth, diversify portfolios, and participate in a transformative economic system. By addressing flaws in traditional financial instruments and providing an alternative to inflationary fiat currencies, Bitcoin has cemented its place as both a store of value and a high-growth asset. However, this innovative financial tool also comes with risks that require careful analysis and informed decision-making.

Why Bitcoin Matters to Personal and Institutional Investors

1. Personal Investors

For individual investors, Bitcoin represents an opportunity to:

- Preserve Wealth:
  Bitcoin's fixed supply of 21 million coins makes it an attractive hedge against inflation and currency devaluation, particularly in regions with unstable fiat currencies.

  Example: In countries like Argentina and Venezuela, individuals have turned to Bitcoin to protect their savings from hyperinflation.

- Achieve Financial Sovereignty:
  Bitcoin allows individuals to own and control their wealth without relying on banks or financial intermediaries. That is especially valuable in regions with unstable banking systems or authoritarian regimes.

- Participate in Growth:
  As an emerging asset class, Bitcoin offers significant growth potential, making it appealing to investors willing to take calculated risks for potentially high rewards.

2. Institutional Investors

For corporations, hedge funds, and institutional players, Bitcoin provides:

- Portfolio Diversification:
  Bitcoin's low correlation with traditional assets like stocks and bonds makes it a valuable addition to diversified investment portfolios, reducing overall risk.

  Example: Fidelity Investments has integrated Bitcoin into its offerings, citing its diversification benefits.

- Inflation Hedge:
  Institutional investors increasingly view Bitcoin as digital gold, offering protection against the devaluation of fiat currencies due to excessive money printing.

- Treasury Strategy:
  Companies like MicroStrategy and Tesla have adopted Bitcoin as a treasury reserve asset, using it to store value and hedge against economic uncertainty.

- Growing Market Acceptance:
  With the approval of spot Bitcoin ETFs and increased regulatory clarity, institutions can now invest in Bitcoin through familiar financial instruments, accelerating adoption.

Risks vs. Rewards

Risks

1. Volatility:
   Bitcoin's price is notoriously volatile, often experiencing swings of 20-30% in a single day. While this creates opportunities for traders, it can be unsettling for long-term investors.

2. Regulatory Uncertainty:
   Governments worldwide are still developing policies around Bitcoin. While increased regulation could bring legitimacy, it may also limit usage or impose taxation.

3. Technological Risks:
   Bitcoin's value relies on its underlying technology. Issues like blockchain forks, potential quantum computing threats, or unforeseen vulnerabilities could pose risks.

4. Environmental Concerns:
   Bitcoin mining consumes a significant amount of energy, drawing criticism for its environmental impact. However, efforts to use renewable energy are mitigating these concerns.

5. Market Manipulation:
   As a relatively young market, Bitcoin is still susceptible to manipulation by large holders or coordinated trading activities.

Rewards

1. High Growth Potential:
   - Bitcoin's historical performance has been extraordinary, with its price increasing from less than $1 in 2010 to an all-time high of $69,000 in 2021, and $103,000 in 2024.
   - Despite its volatility, Bitcoin's long-term trend has been upward, driven by growing adoption and limited supply.

2. Inflation Protection:
   Bitcoin's fixed supply makes it inherently deflationary, offering protection against the erosion of purchasing power caused by inflation.

3. Global Accessibility:
   Bitcoin operates 24/7, with no reliance on traditional banking hours or infrastructure. This borderless nature makes it accessible to anyone, anywhere.

4. Liquidity:
   Bitcoin is one of the most liquid assets in the world, with daily trading volumes exceeding billions of dollars. This ensures that investors can buy or sell Bitcoin easily.

Bitcoin offers a unique investment opportunity for both personal and institutional investors, providing high growth potential, inflation protection, and accessibility unmatched by traditional assets. However, it comes with significant risks, including volatility and regulatory uncertainty, which require careful consideration.

For those who understand its risks and rewards, Bitcoin represents a transformative asset class—challenging traditional notions of value and investment. Its role as a hedge against inflation and a tool for financial sovereignty makes it a compelling addition to any diversified portfolio. Whether as a complement to traditional assets like gold and stocks or as a revolutionary store of value in its own right, Bitcoin has firmly established itself as a cornerstone of the future financial system.

Strategies for Investing in Bitcoin

DCA vs. Lump-Sum Investment

Investing in Bitcoin requires thoughtful strategies to maximize potential returns while managing risks. Two of the most common approaches are Dollar-Cost Averaging (DCA) and lump-sum investment. Each strategy has its advantages and considerations, depending on the investor's financial goals, risk tolerance, and market conditions.

1. Dollar-Cost Averaging (DCA)

What is DCA?
Dollar-Cost Averaging involves investing a fixed amount of money into Bitcoin at regular intervals (e.g., weekly, monthly), regardless of its price. This method spreads purchases over time, reducing the impact of market volatility.

Advantages of DCA:

1. Reduces Emotional Investing:
   Investors don't need to worry about timing the market. DCA eliminates the pressure of deciding the 'perfect' time to buy, reducing emotional decision-making.

2. Mitigates Volatility Risk:
   By buying at different price points, DCA smooths out the effects of Bitcoin's price fluctuations, resulting in an average cost over time.

3. Accessibility:
   DCA is ideal for investors with limited funds, as it allows them to invest small amounts incrementally rather than requiring a large initial outlay.

4. Long-Term Focus:
   Encourages a disciplined, long-term approach to investing, especially for those who believe in Bitcoin's potential for future growth.

Example:

An investor decides to invest $500 per month into Bitcoin. Over the course of a year, they buy Bitcoin at various price levels, averaging their cost and reducing the risk of buying at a peak.

Considerations for DCA:

- Missed Opportunities: If Bitcoin's price rises consistently, DCA may lead to a higher average cost compared to a lump-sum investment made upfront.

- Requires Discipline: Sticking to the plan during volatile periods can be challenging.

2. Lump-Sum Investment

What is Lump-Sum Investment?
A lump-sum investment involves investing a large amount of capital into Bitcoin all at once. This strategy is often selected by investors with significant cash available who believe in Bitcoin's long-term potential.

Advantages of Lump-Sum Investment:

1. Immediate Market Exposure:
   The entire investment is exposed to Bitcoin's potential growth immediately, allowing the investor to benefit from any price increases right away.

2. Simplicity:
   A one-time transaction eliminates the need for ongoing purchases, saving time and effort.

3. Historical Data Support:
   Historically, Bitcoin's price has trended upward over the long term. A lump-sum investment during favorable market conditions could maximize returns.

Example:

An investor has $10,000 and buys Bitcoin in a single transaction when the price is $20,000 per coin. If Bitcoin rises to $40,000, the investment doubles in value.

Considerations for Lump-Sum Investment:

- Higher Risk of Timing the Market:

  A lump-sum investment requires choosing the right moment to enter the market. Buying at a peak could result in significant short-term losses.

- Emotional Stress:

  Investors may experience regret if Bitcoin's price drops shortly after their purchase, potentially leading to panic selling.

The following table shows the differences between DCA and Lump-Sum Investment.

Which Strategy is Right for You?

Factor	DCA	Lump-Sum Investment
Risk Tolerance	Lower risk, spreads entry points	Higher risk, depends on market timing
Investment Amount	Suitable for smaller, regular investments	Best for large, available funds
Volatility Management	Smooths out volatility over time	Exposed to immediate price swings
Market Timing	Reduces importance of timing	Timing is critical
Time Commitment	Requires ongoing commitment	One-time action

Blended Approach

Some investors combine DCA and lump-sum strategies for the best of both worlds.

Example: An investor might make an initial lump-sum purchase to establish a position in Bitcoin, followed by smaller, regular DCA investments to build their holdings over time.

Conclusion

Both DCA and lump-sum investment strategies have their merits, and the choice ultimately depends on the investor's financial situation, market outlook, and risk tolerance.

- DCA is ideal for those seeking a steady, low-stress approach to Bitcoin investment, particularly in volatile markets.
- Lump-sum investment may be better suited for those with strong conviction in Bitcoin's long-term potential and a higher risk tolerance.

Regardless of the strategy chosen, the key to successful investing in Bitcoin is staying informed, disciplined, and aligned with your financial goals.

Long-Term Holding ('HODLing') vs. Active Trading

When investing in Bitcoin, one key decision is whether to adopt a long-term holding strategy (HODLing) or engage in active trading. Each approach offers distinct advantages and challenges, depending on your financial goals, risk tolerance, and market expertise. Let's explore both strategies in detail.

1. Long-Term Holding ('HODLing')

What is HODLing?
HODLing refers to buying Bitcoin and holding onto it for the long term, regardless of short-term price fluctuations. The term originated from a misspelled word ('hold') in a Bitcoin forum post in 2013, which symbolized the expression 'hold on for dear life', and has since become a rallying cry for Bitcoin believers.

Key Principles:

- Focus on Fundamentals: HODLers believe in Bitcoin's long-term potential as a store of value, inflation hedge, or future global reserve currency.
- Ignore Short-Term Volatility: HODLers aim to ride out Bitcoin's price swings, betting that its value will appreciate significantly over time.

Advantages of HODLing:

1. Simplicity:
   HODLing requires minimal effort. Once Bitcoin is purchased, the investor holds it in a secure wallet, avoiding the complexities of frequent trading.

2. Lower Risk of Emotional Decisions:
   By committing to a long-term mindset, HODLers avoid impulsive reactions to short-term market volatility, reducing the likelihood of selling at a loss.

3. Benefiting from Long-Term Trends:
   Historically, Bitcoin's price has trended upward in the long-term, despite periods of sharp corrections. HODLing allows investors to capture the broader growth trend.

4. Tax Efficiency:
   In many jurisdictions, holding Bitcoin for longer periods may result in lower capital gains taxes compared to profits from short-term trading.

Challenges of HODLing:

1. Patience Required:
   HODLing requires a strong belief in Bitcoin's future, even during bear markets when its price may drop significantly.

2. Missed Opportunities:
   HODLers may miss short-term trading opportunities to capitalize on price volatility.

3. Security Risks:
   Long-term holders must take precautions to secure their Bitcoin, as loss of private keys or wallet breaches could result in irretrievable losses.

2. Active Trading

What is Active Trading?
Active trading involves frequently buying and selling Bitcoin to capitalize on short-term price movements. Traders rely on technical analysis, market trends, and timing to profit from volatility.

Key Approaches:

- Day Trading: Buying and selling Bitcoin within the same day to profit from intraday price fluctuations.
- Swing Trading: Holding Bitcoin for a few days or weeks to capitalize on medium-term trends.
- Scalping: Making multiple trades in a day for small, incremental profits.

Advantages of Active Trading:

1. Profit from Volatility:
   Bitcoin's high volatility creates numerous opportunities for traders to profit from price swings.

2. Flexibility:
   Active trading allows investors to adjust their positions quickly based on market conditions and news.

3. Potentially Higher Returns:
   Skilled traders can outperform long-term holders by capitalizing on frequent market movements.

Challenges of Active Trading:

1. Time-Intensive:
   Active trading requires constant monitoring of the market, technical analysis, and quick decision-making.
2. High Risk:
   Frequent trading increases exposure to short-term price swings, which can lead to significant losses, especially for inexperienced traders.

3. Trading Fees:
   Frequent buying and selling incurs transaction fees, which can erode profits over time.

4. Tax Implications:
   In many countries, trading profits are taxed at higher rates than long-term gains, reducing overall returns.

Comparison Table: HODLing vs. Active Trading

Aspect	HODLing	Active Trading
Effort Required	Minimal	High, requires constant monitoring
Risk	Lower, focused on long-term value	Higher, due to market volatility
Returns	Long-term potential, steady growth	Short-term gains, but inconsistent
Tax Implications	Favorable for long-term profits	Short-term profits taxed at higher rates
Emotional Involvement	Minimal, avoids emotional decision making	High, requires quick reactions
Skill Level	Suitable for beginners and experts alike	Best for experienced and knowledgeable traders

Which Strategy is Right for You?

1. Choose HODLing If:
   - You believe in Bitcoin's long-term potential and view it as a store of value or hedge against inflation.
   - You prefer a low-maintenance approach and are not comfortable with frequent trading.
   - You have a long investment horizon and can endure short-term price volatility.
2. Choose Active Trading If:
   - You have experience in financial markets and a solid understanding of technical analysis.
   - You enjoy the challenge of navigating market fluctuations and have the time to monitor prices closely.
   - You're comfortable with higher risk and potential losses in pursuit of short-term gains.
3. Blend the Strategies:
   - Some investors combine both approaches, HODLing a portion of their Bitcoin for long-term growth while actively trading a smaller portion to capitalize on volatility.

Both HODLing and active trading are viable strategies for investing in Bitcoin, each catering to different types of investors. HODLing is ideal for those seeking a simple, long-term approach, while active trading appeals to those with the expertise and appetite for short-term opportunities. Regardless of the chosen strategy, the key to success lies in understanding the risks, staying disciplined, and aligning the approach with your financial goals and risk tolerance.

Diversification and Portfolio Management with Bitcoin

As Bitcoin continues to gain recognition as a legitimate asset class, its role in diversified investment portfolios has become a key area of focus. By incorporating Bitcoin alongside traditional assets like stocks, bonds, and real estate, investors can enhance portfolio performance, manage risk, and align their investments with the evolving financial landscape. However, effective diversification requires thoughtful strategy and portfolio management to balance potential rewards with associated risks.

The Importance of Diversification

Diversification involves spreading investments across various asset classes to minimize risk. The goal is to minimize the impact of poor performance on one asset while maximizing overall portfolio returns. Bitcoin's unique characteristics make it an appealing addition to a diversified portfolio:

1. Low Correlation with Traditional Assets:
   Historically, Bitcoin has shown a low or negative correlation with traditional assets like stocks, bonds, and commodities. This means Bitcoin's price movements often differ from or counteract those of other investments, providing a hedge against market downturns.

2. Growth Potential:
   Bitcoin's historical growth trajectory has outperformed most traditional asset classes, making it an attractive choice for investors seeking high returns.

3. Hedge Against Inflation:
   Bitcoin's fixed supply and decentralized nature make it a potential safeguard against inflation and currency devaluation, especially in economic environments characterized by excessive money printing.

How Bitcoin Fits into a Diversified Portfolio

1. Strategic Allocation

The percentage of Bitcoin in a portfolio should depend on the investor's goals, risk tolerance, and investment horizon:

- Conservative Allocation (1-5%):
  Ideal for risk-averse investors who want exposure to Bitcoin's growth potential without overexposing their portfolio to volatility.

- Moderate Allocation (5-15%):
  Suitable for investors comfortable with some risk, aiming to enhance returns while maintaining stability.

- Aggressive Allocation (15-30%):
  For investors with high-risk tolerance who believe strongly in Bitcoin's long-term potential.

2. Portfolio Examples:

Portfolio Type	Asset Allocation
Conservative	50% Bonds, 40% Stocks, 5% Bitcoin, 5% Gold
Balanced	40% Stocks, 30% Bonds, 15% Bitcoin, 15% Real Estate
Growth-Oriented	50% Stocks, 20% Bitcoin, 15% Tech ETFs, 15% Alternative Investments

Risk Management in a Bitcoin-Integrated Portfolio

1. Volatility Mitigation:
   Bitcoin's price can fluctuate dramatically. By balancing it with more stable assets such as bonds or real estate, investors can help stabilize their portfolios.

2. Periodic Rebalancing:
   As Bitcoin's value grows, its proportion in the portfolio may exceed the target allocation. Periodic rebalancing helps maintain the portfolio's alignment with the investor's risk tolerance and goals.

3. Diversify Within Bitcoin:
   Consider diversifying within the cryptocurrency space by including assets such as Ethereum or stablecoins. However, Bitcoin's dominance and maturity make it the safest and most established crypto investment.

4. Liquidity Considerations:
   Bitcoin's high liquidity ensures that investors can quickly convert holdings into cash, making it an effective tool for maintaining portfolio flexibility.

Portfolio Scenarios: The Bitcoin Effect

1. Enhanced Returns

A study by Fidelity found that adding a small percentage of Bitcoin to a traditional 60/40 portfolio (60% stocks, 40% bonds) increased overall returns without significantly increasing risk.

2. Protection During Economic Uncertainty

During periods of market instability or inflation, Bitcoin's non-sovereign nature and scarcity can serve as a hedge, helping preserve portfolio value.

3. Volatility Challenges

While Bitcoin's high growth potential is appealing, its volatility can amplify portfolio fluctuations. A disciplined approach to allocation and rebalancing is essential.

Common Mistakes to Avoid

1. Overexposure:
   Allocating too much of your portfolio to Bitcoin can lead to excessive risk, especially for inexperienced investors.

2. Chasing Short-Term Gains:
   Bitcoin's price can spike dramatically, leading to FOMO (fear of missing out). Stick to your strategy rather than chasing hype. If you can HOLD for more than four years, it should still be fine, as historical data suggests that prices are likely to rise. However, if you panic due to a price drop and sell your Bitcoins, you may end up losing even your initial investment.

3. Neglecting Security:
   If holding Bitcoin directly, ensure it is stored securely in wallets. Losing access to your private keys could result in irreversible losses.

4. Ignoring Tax Implications:
   Understand the tax laws in your jurisdiction regarding Bitcoin investments, especially for frequent trades or large allocations.

The Future of Bitcoin in Portfolio Management

As Bitcoin matures, its role in portfolio management is expected to expand:

- Institutional Integration:
  With the approval of spot Bitcoin ETFs, more institutional investors are incorporating Bitcoin into pension funds, endowments, and sovereign wealth funds.

- Increased Stability:
  Growing adoption and liquidity may reduce Bitcoin's volatility over time, making it even more attractive for portfolio diversification.

Integrating Bitcoin into a diversified portfolio offers significant opportunities to enhance returns, mitigate inflation risks, and access a transformative asset class. However, effective portfolio management is critical to navigating Bitcoin's volatility and maximizing its benefits.

By allocating strategically, rebalancing regularly, and understanding Bitcoin's unique attributes, investors can harness its potential while maintaining a balanced and resilient investment portfolio. As Bitcoin continues to reshape the financial landscape, its role as a key component of modern portfolio management will likely grow.

Part 7. Getting Started with Bitcoin
How to Buy, Sell, and Trade

Whether you're looking to invest for the long term, trade for short-term gains, or simply explore the world of cryptocurrency, getting started with Bitcoin requires a fundamental understanding of how to buy, sell, and trade it. Here's a comprehensive guide to help you navigate the process.

Setting the Foundation

Understand the Basics

Before diving into Bitcoin, it's essential to understand:

- What Bitcoin Is: Bitcoin is a decentralized digital currency that operates on a peer-to-peer network, eliminating the need for intermediaries.

- The Blockchain: Transactions are recorded on a transparent and immutable ledger.

- Your Goals: Decide whether you're investing long-term, trading short-term, or using Bitcoin as a payment method.

1. How to Buy Bitcoin

Step 1: Cryptocurrency Exchanges

Examples: Coinbase, Binance, or other exchanges based on the country you're living in. These platforms offer a user-friendly way to buy Bitcoin using fiat currencies (e.g., USD, EUR).

Step 2: Set Up an Account

- Provide the required personal information (name, email, and phone number).
- Complete the KYC (Know Your Customer) verification process, which typically involves uploading a valid ID and proof of address.

Step 3: Deposit Funds

- Fund your account using bank transfers, credit/debit cards, or other supported payment methods.

Step 4: Place Your Order

- Market Order: Buys Bitcoin at the current market price.
- Limit Order: Sets a specific price at which you want to buy Bitcoin.

2. How to Sell Bitcoin

Step 1: Choose a Selling Method

1. Exchanges:
   Sell your Bitcoin on platforms like Coinbase or Binance by converting it to fiat or another cryptocurrency.

2. Bitcoin ATMs:
   Some Bitcoin ATMs allow you to sell Bitcoin for cash.

Step 2: Transfer Bitcoin to the Platform

- Move your Bitcoin from your wallet to the exchange or P2P platform.

- Ensure you send the exact amount to the correct wallet address to avoid errors.

Step 3: Execute the Sale

- Decide whether to sell at market price or set a limit order for your desired price.

- Once the sale is complete, transfer your fiat funds to your bank account.

3. Be Your Own Bank
Securing Bitcoin: Custody and Security Best Practices

When stepping into the world of Bitcoin, security is paramount. Unlike traditional financial systems, Bitcoin gives you complete ownership of your wealth—but with that freedom comes significant responsibility. One of the most critical decisions you'll face is choosing between self-custody and custodial solutions for managing your Bitcoin.

Self-Custody: Be Your Own Bank

Self-custody means you control your private keys, the cryptographic codes that grant access to your Bitcoin. Without these keys, your Bitcoin is inaccessible—even to you. While self-custody offers unparalleled security and independence, it also requires diligence and knowledge.

Benefits of Self-Custody:

1. Full Ownership: You are the sole custodian of your Bitcoin, ensuring no third party can freeze, confiscate, or lose your funds.
2. Enhanced Security: Properly managed self-custody reduces the risk of centralized breaches or hacks.
3. Privacy: Your Bitcoin holdings remain private, as no third-party service has visibility into your balance or transactions.

Best Practices for Self-Custody:

1. Use a Hardware Wallet: Devices like Ledger, Tangem or Trezor keep your private keys offline, protecting them from cyber threats.
2. Backup Your Recovery Phrase: Write down the 12- or 24-word recovery phrase in multiple secure locations. Avoid storing it digitally.
3. Secure Storage: Use fireproof safes or other protective measures for physical backups.
4. Stay Vigilant: Avoid phishing scams, fake wallet applications, and sharing sensitive information.
5. You can find tutorial videos on YouTube that guide you through setting up and managing these wallets. You can find videos on my Channels, or YouTube in general.

Custodial Solutions: Trusting Third Parties

Custodial solutions involve entrusting a third-party service, such as an exchange or a digital wallet provider, to manage your private keys. While this is more convenient, it introduces risks associated with centralization.

Benefits of Custodial Solutions:

- Ease of Use: Perfect for beginners not familiar with handling private keys.
- Accessibility: Often provides additional services like trading, staking, and customer support.
- Backup Assistance: Reduces the risk of losing funds due to mismanaged recovery phrases.

Risks of Custodial Solutions:

- Counterparty Risk: If the provider is hacked, goes bankrupt, or acts maliciously, your funds may be at risk.
- Lack of Control: You rely on the service to act responsibly and keep your Bitcoin safe.

Best Practices for Custodial Solutions:

- Choose Reputable Providers: Use well-known and regulated platforms with strong security measures.
- Enable Two-Factor Authentication (2FA): Add an extra layer of protection to your account.
- Diversify: Avoid storing all your Bitcoin in one custodial account.
- Withdraw to Self-Custody: For long-term holdings, consider moving your funds to a self-custody solution.

Making the Right Choice

Your choice between self-custody and custodial solutions depends on your level of expertise, security needs, and how frequently you transact. For Bitcoin newcomers, starting with a reliable custodial service can be a practical choice. However, as your understanding deepens, transitioning to self-custody offers enhanced security and independence.

Remember: 'Not your keys, not your coins.' Educate yourself, remain vigilant, and prioritize security to safeguard your financial freedom.

4. Common Mistakes to Avoid

1. Investing Without Research:
   Understand Bitcoin and the platforms you're using before investing.

2. Falling for Scams:
   Be cautious of unsolicited offers, phishing emails, and fake giveaways.

3. Neglecting Security:
   Failing to secure your wallet or account can result in a permanent loss of funds.

4. Overtrading:
   Trading frequently without a clear strategy can lead to significant losses.

Buying, selling, and trading Bitcoin has become more accessible than ever, thanks to the increasing number of platforms and resources available. By understanding the process and taking necessary precautions, you can navigate through the Bitcoin market with confidence.

Whether you're a long-term investor or a short-term trader, starting with Bitcoin requires careful planning, continuous learning, and a focus on security. As Bitcoin continues to shape the financial landscape, those who approach it strategically will be well-positioned to benefit from its growth.

5. Bitcoins Road to $1 Million

Bitcoin has captivated the financial world with its meteoric rise in value, turning early adopters into millionaires and sparking widespread speculation about its ultimate price potential. The possibility of Bitcoin reaching $1 million per coin—or even higher, potentially up to $13 million (by Michael Saylor)—cannot be ignored. This bold potential is grounded in its unique characteristics: a fixed supply, increasing institutional adoption, and its role as a hedge against inflation.

However, while the roadmap to these valuations is compelling, it is essential to acknowledge that no outcome is guaranteed. Market conditions, regulatory developments, and unforeseen technological or geopolitical challenges could all influence Bitcoin's trajectory. Let's break down the key drivers and challenges on Bitcoin's road to millions.

A. Bitcoin's Scarcity and Market Dynamics

Fixed Supply: Digital Scarcity
- Bitcoin's supply is capped at 21 million coins, a limit enforced by its blockchain protocol. This finite supply creates digital scarcity, similar to gold, but with even more predictability and certainty.
- With over 19 million Bitcoin already mined, the remaining supply is diminishing, particularly as halvings (events that reduce mining rewards by half) continue to limit new Bitcoin entering circulation.
- Approximately 3.5 Million Bitcoins have been lost in wallets.

Rising Demand vs. Limited Supply
- As institutional adoption increases and retail investors accumulate Bitcoin, demand is expected to significantly outpace supply.
- Unlike fiat currencies, which central banks can print in unlimited quantities, Bitcoin's supply dynamics favor long-term price appreciation.

Understanding Bitcoin Supply Shock and Market Impacts

A Bitcoin supply shock occurs when the available Bitcoin supply in circulation becomes significantly constrained, creating increased competition among buyers. This phenomenon often drives up prices as demand outpaces supply. Several factors contribute to supply shocks in the Bitcoin market:

1. **Halving Events**: Approximately every four years, Bitcoin undergoes a halving event, where the reward given to miners for processing transactions is reduced by 50%. This process cuts the flow of new Bitcoin entering the market. For example, the most recent halving in April 2024 reduced the block reward from 6.25 BTC to 3.125 BTC, tightening the supply pipeline.

2. **Institutional Accumulation**: The approval of Bitcoin spot ETFs and growing institutional interest have led to significant purchases of Bitcoin for long-term holdings. For example, these funds have accumulated significant Bitcoin reserves, decreasing the amount available for trading.

3. **Increased Long-Term Holding**: More Bitcoin holders are transferring their assets from exchanges to personal wallets. This shift signals increased confidence in Bitcoin's future value and removes liquidity from the market, reducing the available supply for day-to-day trading.

These factors together limit Bitcoin's circulating supply, creating conditions where even small increases in demand can have a significant impact on its price.

Current Bitcoin Supply on Exchanges

The amount of Bitcoin held on exchanges provides crucial insights into the market's liquidity and potential for a supply shock. A steady decline in exchange balances reflects increased storage in private wallets, reducing selling pressure and signaling bullish sentiment.

As of December 2024, approximately **1,095,026 Bitcoins** remain on exchanges, representing around 5.59% of the total circulating supply. This trend underscores growing confidence in Bitcoin's long-term potential as more investors opt to hold their assets securely offline.

Visualizing the Trend

The following chart depicts the declining trend of Bitcoin balances on exchanges over the past months or years, emphasizing the shift toward long-term holding and its implications for the market.

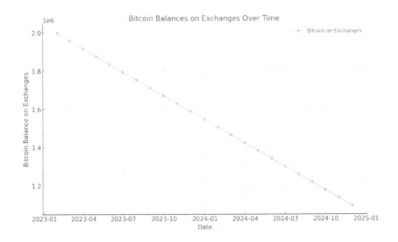

Bitcoin Balances on Exchanges Over Time

B. Macroeconomic Factors Driving Bitcoin's Value

Hedge Against Inflation

In an era of unprecedented monetary expansion, Bitcoin's fixed supply positions it as a hedge against inflation. More and more investors are viewing Bitcoin as 'digital gold,' seeing it as a safeguard against currency devaluation.

Example: The purchasing power of the U.S. dollar has declined by 97% over the last century. Bitcoin's scarcity offers an alternative to fiat currencies subject to inflationary pressures.

Global Economic Uncertainty

Economic instability, geopolitical tensions, and declining trust in central banks drive demand for decentralized, non-sovereign assets like Bitcoin.

Example: Countries experiencing hyperinflation (e.g., Venezuela, Turkey) or economic sanctions (e.g., Russia) have seen Bitcoin adoption surge as citizens seek financial independence.

Institutional Adoption and Wealth Transfer

As institutional players like BlackRock, MicroStrategy, and Tesla increase their Bitcoin holdings, the perception of Bitcoin as a legitimate asset grows.

Additionally, trillions of dollars are projected to shift from baby boomers to younger, tech-savvy generations, who are more likely to embrace Bitcoin as a core asset.

C. Mathematical Path to $1 Million

Market Capitalization

Market capitalization (Market Cap) represents the total value of all Bitcoins in circulation.

Bitcoin's price is a function of its market capitalization divided by the circulating supply.
Market Cap = Price × Supply.

For example, if the price of Bitcoin is $50,000 and the circulating supply is 19 million BTC then we have a market capitalization of:
$950 billion = $50,000 (price) × 19,000,000 (coins).

For Bitcoin to reach $1 million, the market capitalization must be:
$21 trillion = $1 million × 21 million coins.

While this figure may seem staggering, it represents a fraction of the global wealth in traditional assets.

Comparing Bitcoin's Market Cap to Other Assets

To contextualize this figure, consider the current market values of other major asset classes:

- Gold: ~$13 trillion.
- Global Real Estate: ~$327 trillion.
- Global Equities: ~$117 trillion.

If Bitcoin captures even 5-10% of these markets, $1 million per coin becomes feasible.

There is also the global debt: ~$300 trillion.

For Bitcoin to achieve a $21 trillion market cap, it would need to capture approximately:

- 160% of gold's current market cap, or
- 6.4% of the global real estate market, or
- 7% of the worldwide debt market.

These figures highlight that Bitcoin's potential is not just plausible, but achievable within the broader context of global asset reallocation.

Adoption Curve

Bitcoin adoption follows a classic S-curve, similar to transformative technologies like the internet. Currently, Bitcoin adoption is estimated at 4-5% of the global population, leaving significant room for growth.

D. Key Drivers to $1 Million

Institutional Inflows

The approval of spot Bitcoin ETFs has opened the floodgates for institutional capital. As pensions, endowments, and sovereign wealth funds allocate even a small percentage of their portfolios to Bitcoin, demand could skyrocket.

Global Reserve Asset Potential

Bitcoin's neutrality, scarcity, and portability make it a candidate for a global reserve asset, particularly as trust in traditional reserve currencies like the U.S. dollar wanes.

Network Effects

Bitcoin's value is strengthened by its expanding user base and increasing utility:

- Increased adoption drives higher demand.
- Expanding use cases (e.g., remittances, payments) enhance its functionality and appeal.

E. Success Scenarios for $1 Million Bitcoin

- Global Adoption:

If Bitcoin becomes widely accepted as a store of value, medium of exchange, and unit of account, its market cap could rival or exceed gold.

- Sovereign Wealth and Reserve Adoption:

Countries and central banks allocating reserves to Bitcoin could significantly increase demand.

For example, 1% of global sovereign wealth (approx. $12 trillion) would inject $120 billion into Bitcoin, potentially driving its price higher.

- Hyperbitcoinization:

A theoretical scenario where Bitcoin replaces fiat currencies as the dominant medium of exchange, resulting in exponential price appreciation.

F. The Role of Halvings in Bitcoin's Price Trajectory

Bitcoin's halving events, which occur approximately every four years, reduce the mining reward by half, creating a deflationary effect:

- 2024 Halving: Expected to reduce daily Bitcoin issuance, increasing scarcity.
- Historically, halvings have preceded major bull runs, as seen in 2012, 2016, and 2020.

Bitcoin's path to $1 million or higher is entirely possible but not guaranteed. Frequently called the 'new gold' or 'digital gold,' Bitcoin has solidified its position as a revolutionary asset class. Its groundbreaking technology, increasing global adoption, and unique scarcity make it unlike any asset in history.

With expectations of widespread adoption continuing to grow and its finite supply creating unparalleled scarcity, Bitcoin's value has the potential to surpass $1 million. While the journey is not without its challenges, Bitcoin remains one of the most promising and transformative financial innovations of the 21st century.

6. The Math Behind Bitcoin's Scarcity and Market Cap

Bitcoin's value proposition is deeply rooted in its scarcity and the mechanics of its market capitalization. By design, Bitcoin's fixed supply and decentralized protocol create a predictable economic framework that differentiates it from traditional fiat currencies and other financial assets. Grasping the mathematics behind Bitcoin's scarcity and market cap is crucial to understanding its potential as both a store of value and an investment asset.

A. Market Capitalization: Measuring Bitcoin's Value

As mentioned above, market capitalization represents the total value of all Bitcoin in circulation:

Market Cap = Current Price × Circulating Supply

Bitcoin's market capitalization increase is usually associated with higher demand and a rise in price, but external factors such as supply, regulatory policy, and investor psychology must be taken into account.

B. The Scarcity Formula and Demand Dynamics

Stock-to-Flow Model

The Stock-to-Flow (S2F) model is a popular framework for valuing Bitcoin based on its scarcity:
- Stock: The total existing supply of Bitcoin.
- Flow: The annual new supply (from mining rewards).
- S2F Ratio: Stock ÷ Flow.

Higher S2F ratios indicate greater scarcity.

Bitcoin's Current S2F Ratio:
- Stock: ~19.5 million BTC.
- Flow: ~328,500 BTC per year (pre-halving).
- S2F = 19,500,000 ÷ 328,500 ≈ 59.3.
- 2024 Post-Halving, the annual flow will be halved, doubling the S2F ratio to approximately 118.6, surpassing gold's current S2F ratio of ~62.

Impact on Price

The S2F model suggests that as Bitcoin's scarcity increases with each halving, its value will probably rise, assuming demand remains constant or grows.

C. Supply vs. Demand: The Driving Force

Supply Constraints

- Unlike fiat currencies, where central banks can print unlimited amounts, Bitcoin's fixed supply ensures that scarcity will always play a central role in its valuation.
- As more Bitcoin is lost or held for long-term investment, the available supply for trading decreases, intensifying scarcity.

Demand Growth

- Institutional Adoption: Companies like Microstrategy, BlackRock, are adding Bitcoin to their balance sheets.
- Bitcoin Reserve From Governments.
- Retail Growth: More individuals view Bitcoin as a hedge against inflation and a store of value.
- Global Utility: Bitcoin's use as a medium of exchange and remittance tool is growing in developing economies.

D. Price Projections Based on Market Cap
Scenarios for Bitcoin's Price
Path to $1 Million+

Market Cap	Price per Bitcoin
$1 trillion	$47,619
$5 trillion	$238,095
$10 trillion	$476,190
$21 trillion	$1,000,000
$50 trillion	$2,380,952

For Bitcoin to reach $1 million, the following significant capital inflows would be needed:

- Institutional investors reallocate portions of gold, equities, or bonds to Bitcoin.
- Sovereign wealth funds and central banks adopt Bitcoin as a reserve asset.
- Widespread retail adoption as an inflation hedge and store of value.

7. Factors That Could Drive or Hinder Bitcoin's Price Growth

Bitcoin's price is shaped by a complex interaction of various factors, ranging from macroeconomic conditions to technological developments and regulatory environments. Understanding these drivers and barriers is essential for assessing its future potential.

Factors Driving Bitcoin's Price Growth

1. Increasing Institutional Adoption

- Spot Bitcoin ETFs: The approval of spot Bitcoin ETFs, including those by BlackRock and Fidelity, has made Bitcoin more accessible to institutional investors. These funds bring legitimacy and massive capital inflows.
- Corporate Treasury Investments: Companies like MicroStrategy and Tesla have adopted Bitcoin as a treasury reserve asset, inspiring others to follow suit.
- Hedge Funds and Sovereign Wealth Funds: Large institutional players are beginning to view Bitcoin as a hedge against inflation and geopolitical risk.

2. Global Economic Uncertainty

- Inflation Hedge: As fiat currencies lose value due to inflation, Bitcoin's fixed supply makes it an attractive alternative for preserving purchasing power.
- Geopolitical Crises: In regions experiencing political instability or sanctions, Bitcoin offers a censorship-resistant means of transacting and storing wealth.

Example: Bitcoin adoption has surged in countries like Venezuela and Turkey, where local currencies have experienced hyperinflation.

3. Technological Developments

- Scaling Solutions: Innovations like the Lightning Network enhance Bitcoin's scalability, enabling faster and cheaper transactions, which broadens its utility.
- Energy Efficiency Improvements: Efforts to shift Bitcoin mining to renewable energy sources address environmental concerns, increasing acceptance.
- Improved Security Features: Advances in hardware wallets and custody solutions make Bitcoin more secure and appealing to individuals and institutions.

4. Increasing Regulatory Clarity

- Pro-Crypto Regulations: Countries like Switzerland, Singapore, and the U.S. (with recent ETF approvals) are establishing clear regulatory frameworks, boosting investor confidence.
- Central Bank Interest: Some central banks, as those in Russia and Iran, have explored Bitcoin for international trade, signaling potential future adoption.

5. Cultural and Generational Shifts

- Millennial and Gen Z Interest: Younger generations, who are more tech-savvy and distrustful of traditional financial systems, are embracing Bitcoin as a new standard for wealth.
- Global Financial Literacy: Growing awareness and education about Bitcoin's benefits drive adoption across diverse demographics.

6. Scarcity and Market Dynamics

- Halvings: Bitcoin's programmed supply reductions (halvings) decrease the rate of new Bitcoin entering circulation, creating upward price pressure.
- Network Effects: As more people adopt Bitcoin, its value increases due to its growing utility and acceptance.

Factors Hindering Bitcoin's Price Growth

1. Regulatory Risks

- Bans or Restrictions: Some governments, like China, have implemented strict bans on Bitcoin mining and trading. Similar actions in other countries could dampen adoption.
- Tax Policies: Aggressive taxation of Bitcoin gains or transactions could discourage investment.
- Central Bank Digital Currencies (CBDCs): Governments may promote CBDCs as alternatives to Bitcoin, potentially limiting its use as a medium of exchange.

2. Market Volatility

- Bitcoin's price is notoriously volatile, which can deter risk-averse investors and prevent its adoption as a stable store of value or medium of exchange.

3. Technological Risks

- Blockchain Scalability: While solutions like the Lightning Network exist, Bitcoin's base layer remains limited in transaction throughput, which could hinder mass adoption.
- Quantum Computing Threats: Advances in quantum computing could theoretically undermine Bitcoin's cryptographic security, though no immediate threats are known.

4. Competition

- Other Cryptocurrencies: Competing digital assets, such as Ethereum, Solana, or even emerging projects, may divert investment and attention from Bitcoin.
- Tokenized Assets: The rise of tokenized real estate, equities, and commodities may provide alternative investment opportunities.

5. Speculation and Manipulation

- Whale Activity: Large holders ('whales') can manipulate markets, creating instability and uncertainty for smaller investors.
- Exchanges: Lack of transparency or liquidity on some cryptocurrency exchanges can contribute to price manipulation.

6. Public Perception and Education

- Misinformation: Negative media coverage or misconceptions about Bitcoin can deter new investors. Over time this has changed, especially in the last 12 months and after the Bitcoin ETF approval.
- Complexity: Understanding Bitcoin requires a basic knowledge of blockchain technology and financial principles, which can be a barrier to entry for some. This problem is being solved every day by more and more people educating others, with the internet and social media playing an increasingly important role in spreading this knowledge.

Balancing the Forces

- Bitcoin's core attributes — scarcity, decentralization, and global accessibility — position it as a unique asset in a rapidly evolving financial ecosystem.

- Institutional adoption and technological advancements continue to drive momentum, while cultural shifts favor its long-term growth.

The factors driving and hindering Bitcoin's price growth reflect the dynamic nature of this transformative asset. While the path to higher valuations is not without obstacles, Bitcoin's underlying principles and growing acceptance provide a strong foundation for its continued evolution. For investors, understanding these forces is key to navigating the opportunities and challenges that define Bitcoin's future.

Part 8. Bitcoin's Societal Impact Empowering Individuals in Countries with Unstable Currencies

Bitcoin's potential to transform societies is perhaps most evident in regions grappling with unstable currencies, hyperinflation, and limited access to traditional banking systems. By offering a decentralized, borderless, and censorship-resistant alternative, Bitcoin empowers individuals to take control of their financial futures, even in the face of economic turmoil and government mismanagement.

1. The Problem: Unstable Currencies and Economic Challenges

Hyperinflation and Currency Devaluation

In countries like Venezuela, Zimbabwe, and Argentina, hyperinflation has rendered local currencies virtually worthless, eroding citizens' savings and purchasing power overnight.

Example: Venezuela's inflation rate exceeded 10 million percent in 2019, leading to a collapse in confidence in the bolívar.

Example: Zimbabwe experienced such severe hyperinflation that citizens were forced to use foreign currencies, like the U.S. dollar, for everyday transactions.

Restricted Access to Banking

Many people in developing economies lack access to traditional banking systems. According to the World Bank, over 1.4 billion adults globally remain unbanked.

Factors contributing to this include high banking fees, geographic inaccessibility, and mistrust of financial institutions.

Capital Controls and Censorship

In some countries, governments impose capital controls restricting citizens' ability to move money internationally or access foreign currencies.

Example: In Turkey, strict capital controls have limited citizens' ability to protect their wealth as the lira continues to lose value.

2. Bitcoin as a Solution

Bitcoin provides an alternative financial system that addresses many of the challenges posed by unstable currencies and traditional banking systems.

Decentralization and Financial Sovereignty

Bitcoin operates on a decentralized network, free from government or institutional control. That ensures that individuals retain full ownership of their wealth, making it immune to confiscation or devaluation by central authorities.

Inflation Hedge

Bitcoin's fixed supply of 21 million coins protects it from inflationary pressures. For citizens in hyperinflationary economies, converting savings into Bitcoin offers a way to preserve purchasing power.

Borderless Transactions

Bitcoin enables individuals to send and receive money across borders without the need for intermediaries or high fees. That is particularly valuable for:

- Remittances: Migrants sending money home to family members.
- Refugees: Individuals fleeing economic or political crises, often losing access to traditional banking systems.

Accessibility

Bitcoin can be accessed with a smartphone and an internet connection, making it a lifeline for unbanked populations. Mobile-based wallets allow users to securely save, transact, and store wealth, without depending on traditional banks.

3. Real-World Examples of Bitcoin's Societal Impact

Venezuela: Survival Amid Hyperinflation

As Venezuela's bolívar collapsed, Bitcoin emerged as a preferred method for preserving wealth and conducting transactions.

- Platforms like LocalBitcoins saw a surge in trading volume as citizens turned to Bitcoin to bypass capital controls and access a stable store of value.

- Some Venezuelans even use Bitcoin to purchase essential goods online, such as food and medicine, that are unavailable locally.

Nigeria: Empowering the Unbanked

Despite government attempts to restrict cryptocurrency use, Nigeria has become a global leader in Bitcoin adoption.

- Over 30% of Nigerians reported using cryptocurrencies in 2022, driven by inflation, unemployment, and limited banking access.

- Bitcoin offers Nigerians a way to receive remittances, pay for services, and hedge against the naira's depreciation.

El Salvador: Legal Tender Experiment

In 2021, El Salvador became the first country to adopt Bitcoin as legal tender.

- The government launched the Chivo Wallet, enabling citizens to transact in Bitcoin without fees.

- While the initiative faced criticism and challenges, it highlighted Bitcoin's potential to integrate unbanked populations into the digital economy.

Advancing Education

As Bitcoin's presence grows, initiatives to educate populations about its benefits, risks, and proper usage are essential to maximizing its societal impact.

Improving Scalability

Innovations like the Lightning Network are making Bitcoin transactions faster and cheaper, increasing its utility in everyday transactions.

Bitcoin's societal impact is most significant in regions with unstable currencies, where it offers a lifeline for individuals seeking to protect their wealth and access the global economy. By offering decentralization, inflation resistance, and financial sovereignty, Bitcoin empowers people to overcome the limitations of traditional economic systems.

While challenges such as volatility and regulatory hurdles persist, Bitcoin's potential to drive financial inclusion and economic empowerment remains undeniable. As adoption grows and education spreads, Bitcoin could transform the lives of millions in underserved and unstable economies, redefining the future of money and access to wealth.

Part 9. Volatility and Market Manipulation

How They Affect Bitcoin's Adoption and Perception

Bitcoin is both celebrated and criticized for its price volatility. While its dramatic price swings have created life-changing wealth for early adopters and traders, they also raise concerns among investors, regulators, and the public. Similarly, the relatively young and unregulated nature of the cryptocurrency market makes it susceptible to manipulation, further influencing Bitcoin's adoption and reputation. Let's explore how these dynamics shape Bitcoin's journey as a financial asset.

1. Understanding Bitcoin's Volatility

What Causes Bitcoin's Price Volatility?

1. Supply and Demand Imbalance:
   - Bitcoin's fixed supply of 21 million coins contrasts with fluctuating demand, creating significant price swings as interest ebbs and flows.
   - Events like halvings, new adoption milestones, or regulatory developments often spark rapid shifts in demand.

2. Speculation-Driven Market:
   - A significant portion of Bitcoin's trading volume comes from speculative investors seeking short-term gains, amplifying price fluctuations.
   - FOMO (Fear of Missing Out) and panic selling often dominate market sentiment.

3. Liquidity Challenges:
   - Compared to traditional markets like stocks or forex, Bitcoin's market is smaller and has fewer participants. This means that large trades or sudden spikes in trading volume can have a disproportionate impact on the price.

4. News and Social Media Influence:
   - Headlines about regulatory crackdowns, institutional adoption, or influential figures like Elon Musk can cause significant price swings.
   - Social media platforms like Twitter and Reddit amplify these effects, creating rapid market movements.

Examples of Volatility in Action

- 2017 Bull Run: Bitcoin's price surged from ~$1,000 in January to nearly $20,000 in December, driven by retail investor enthusiasm and ICO mania.

- 2022 Crash: After reaching an all-time high of $69,000 in November 2021, Bitcoin's price fell below $30,000 by mid-2022 due to regulatory fears and macroeconomic uncertainty.

2. The Impact of Volatility on Adoption

Advantages of Volatility

1. Opportunities for Traders:
   High volatility attracts professional traders who profit from short-term price swings, adding liquidity to the market.

2. Attention and Publicity:
   Price spikes often generate media coverage, sparking curiosity and bringing new participants into the ecosystem.

Challenges Posed by Volatility

1. Hindrance to Everyday Use:
   For Bitcoin to function as a currency, its value must be stable enough for merchants and consumers to trust its purchasing power. Volatility undermines this use case.

   Example: A coffee shop pricing a latte at 0.0003 BTC might find that price significantly undervalued or overvalued within hours.

2. Deterring Institutional Adoption:
   Risk-averse institutions may hesitate to adopt Bitcoin due to concerns about extreme price fluctuations and the potential for short-term losses.

3. Negative Perception:
   Critics often cite volatility as evidence that Bitcoin is a speculative asset rather than a reliable store of value, undermining its reputation as 'digital gold.'

3. Market Manipulation: A Challenge for a Young Market

How Market Manipulation Occurs

1. Whale Activity:
   Large holders of Bitcoin, known as 'whales,' can influence the market by executing massive buy or sell orders.

   Example: A whale selling a large quantity of Bitcoin on a single exchange can trigger panic selling, causing prices to drop.

2. Pump-and-Dump Schemes:
   Coordinated efforts to artificially inflate Bitcoin's price (pump) before selling at the peak (dump) can mislead inexperienced investors.

This is how it works: A group (or even an individual) coordinates a campaign to artificially increase demand and begins buying up large quantities of the cryptocurrency, driving up the price and luring unsuspecting investors. When the price reaches a high level, the organizers of this scheme sell the cryptocurrency en masse. This results in a sharp drop in price and large losses for those who bought it at a high price.

3. Exchange Practices:
   Some exchanges engage in wash trading (fictitious trades to inflate volume) or fail to prevent insider trading, undermining market integrity.

4. Key Opinion Leaders:
   Posts by influential figures, whether intentional or not, can manipulate market sentiment and lead to significant price movements.

Example of Manipulation

The Elon Musk Effect:
In 2021, Tesla CEO Elon Musk's tweets about Bitcoin and Dogecoin caused wild swings in their prices, demonstrating how individual influencers can move markets.

The Wyckoff Accumulation: Understanding Bitcoin's Market Cycles

The Wyckoff Accumulation method, developed by early 20th-century stock market technician Richard D. Wyckoff, is one of the most insightful frameworks for understanding market cycles. Originally designed for traditional financial markets, the Wyckoff Accumulation has proven highly relevant to Bitcoin and cryptocurrency markets, where volatility and speculative behavior dominate.

This part delves into the principles of the Wyckoff methodology, how it applies to Bitcoin, and how investors can use it to identify accumulation phases and make informed decisions.

1. What is the Wyckoff Accumulation?

A. Overview

Wyckoff Accumulation is a market phase where large investors (or 'smart money') accumulate assets like Bitcoin over time, preparing for the next upward price movement.

This phase typically occurs after a bear market or during periods of low public interest, as these conditions allow large investors to accumulate without significantly driving up the price.

B. The Wyckoff Market Cycle

Wyckoff identified four key phases in a market cycle:

1. **Accumulation**: Smart money buys assets at low prices, building positions quietly.
2. **Markup**: Prices begin to rise as demand outweighs supply.
3. **Distribution**: Smart money sells its holdings at high prices to latecomers.
4. **Markdown**: Prices fall as demand decreases, leading to a bear market.

2. Anatomy of the Accumulation Phase

A. Key Features

1. Sideways Trading Range:
   Bitcoin's price moves within a horizontal range, with neither a clear uptrend nor downtrend.

   This range is marked by a support level (the lower boundary) and a resistance level (the upper boundary).

2. Volume Decline:
   Trading volumes typically decrease, signaling reduced public interest and fewer speculative trades.

3. Shakeouts (Spring Phase):
   Sudden price dips below support levels are designed to shake out weak hands (retail investors) and accumulate Bitcoin at lower prices.

   These moves often scare investors into selling, allowing large buyers to scoop up assets cheaply.

B. Stages of Accumulation

The accumulation phase is divided into distinct phases A–E in Wyckoff's model:

Phase A: Stopping the Downtrend

   Bitcoin's downward momentum slows as selling pressure decreases.

   Smart money begins testing the market by buying small amounts.

Phase B: Building the Base

   Bitcoin trades sideways as large investors accumulate gradually.

   This phase can last weeks or months, depending on market conditions.

Phase C: The Spring

   A final shakeout occurs, pushing Bitcoin below the trading range temporarily.

   This move creates a 'bear trap,' luring in short sellers before the price rebounds sharply.

Phase D: Breakout and Retest

> Bitcoin breaks above the resistance level, signaling the start of a new uptrend.

> The price often retests the resistance level, now acting as support.

Phase E: The Markup

> Bitcoin enters a sustained upward trend as demand overwhelms supply.

3. Why the Wyckoff Accumulation Matters for Bitcoin

A. Bitcoin's Volatile Nature

Bitcoin's high volatility and speculative market participants make it an ideal candidate for Wyckoff analysis.

Large investors like institutions and whales use accumulation strategies to capitalize on retail investors' fear and impatience.

B. Historical Examples

1. **2018–2019 Accumulation**:

> After the 2018 bear market, Bitcoin traded between $3,000 and $4,000 for months.

> The accumulation phase ended in early 2019, triggering a bull run that pushed Bitcoin to $13,000.

2. **2020 Accumulation**:

> During the COVID-19 market crash, Bitcoin briefly dropped below $5,000 before entering a prolonged accumulation phase.

This phase led to the 2021 bull market, where Bitcoin reached an all-time high of $69,000.

C. Tools for Identifying Accumulation

1. **Volume Analysis**:
   Watch for declining volume during the trading range and sudden spikes during shakeouts.

2. **Price Action**:
   Identify the support and resistance levels of the trading range.

3. **On-Chain Metrics**:
   Monitor metrics like **whale activity** (large wallets accumulating Bitcoin) and exchange outflows (Bitcoin moving into cold storage).

4. Strategies for Investors

A. Accumulate During the Range

Investors can buy Bitcoin incrementally within the accumulation range, focusing on support levels and avoiding emotional reactions to shakeouts.

B. Beware of False Breakouts

Not all breakouts from the accumulation range signal the start of a bull run. Some are **bull traps**, where prices briefly rise before falling back.

C. Combine with Other Indicators

Use the Wyckoff Accumulation in conjunction with other tools like:

- Relative Strength Index (RSI): To gauge whether Bitcoin is oversold.
- Moving Averages: To confirm trend direction.

5. Risks and Limitations

A. Market Manipulation

Large players (whales) may intentionally create false signals to mislead retail investors.

B. Time Uncertainty

The accumulation phase can last weeks, months, or even years, making it difficult to predict when the breakout will occur.

C. External Factors

Macro events like regulatory announcements or global crises can disrupt the accumulation process.

The Wyckoff Accumulation provides a powerful framework for understanding Bitcoin's price movements, particularly in sideways markets. By recognizing the signs of accumulation, investors can position themselves to capitalize on the next bull run while avoiding common pitfalls like emotional selling during shakeouts.

Bitcoin's past market cycles demonstrate that accumulation phases often precede explosive growth. For those with patience and a long-term perspective, understanding Wyckoff's principles can provide a significant edge in navigating Bitcoin's volatile yet rewarding landscape.

4. Mitigating Volatility and Manipulation

Improved Market Maturity

As Bitcoin adoption grows, increased liquidity and broader participation can reduce price volatility. For example:

- The introduction of spot Bitcoin ETFs has brought more institutional capital into the market, stabilizing prices.

- Greater integration with traditional financial systems can enhance market efficiency.

Technology and Security

- Decentralized exchanges (DEXs) and blockchain analytics tools can help identify and mitigate manipulation.

- Enhancing the robustness of trading platforms can reduce vulnerabilities to whale activity and other exploitative practices.

5. Navigating Volatility and Manipulation

For Investors

1. Long-Term Perspective:

   Volatility is less significant over a long time horizon. Investors focused on Bitcoin's long-term potential may benefit from HODLing strategies.

2. Diversification:

   Allocating only a portion of one's portfolio to Bitcoin can balance the risks of volatility and manipulation.

For Institutions

1. Risk Management Tools:

   Using derivatives like options and futures can hedge against Bitcoin's price swings.

2. Gradual Entry:

   Dollar-cost averaging (DCA) allows institutions to build positions over time, reducing exposure to short-term price fluctuations.

Bitcoin's volatility and susceptibility to market manipulation are frequently cited as obstacles to broader adoption, yet they are also symptoms of its status as an emerging asset class. Over time, as the market matures and regulatory frameworks solidify, these issues are likely to diminish.

For now, volatility continues to attract traders seeking high returns, while manipulation underscores the need for transparency and oversight. By understanding these dynamics, retail and institutional investors can navigate Bitcoin's challenges and leverage its potential as a transformative financial asset.

Part 10. How Bitcoin & Crypto Changed My Life

My Bitcoin Route to Success

In 2012, I heard about Bitcoin for the first time from a friend. He told me I could mine Bitcoin with just $20 in electricity, and the value of one Bitcoin at that time was $30. The 50% profit in a month sounded like an amazing opportunity. He explained that we could rent a computer online that would mine one Bitcoin per month through a company, and I decided to give it a shot. I didn't understand much beyond this. I mined my first Bitcoin but lost it because I didn't know how to store or secure it properly. Back then, I had zero knowledge about wallets or the technology behind Bitcoin.

In 2016, Bitcoin came back into my life when I heard its price was about $600. At that time, I decided to invest again, but it took me three months to set up an account, complete the KYC process, and finally purchase. I bought 0.23 Bitcoin for $250. By 2017, I started diversifying, buying Litecoin, Ethereum, and other altcoins. By the end of 2017, I sold everything during the bull run and made $5,500 in profit, having only invested $850. It felt like a big win, but I still didn't fully understand the technology or its potential.

During the 2017-2018 bull run, I began learning more about Bitcoin, though it was still in its early days. There wasn't much information available in Greek, and I didn't have much money to invest. I held onto a small amount of Bitcoin and a few altcoins, but I wasn't sure if the market would recover or grow. Meanwhile, I focused on developing e-commerce businesses and an e-learning platform.

When the pandemic hit in March 2020, I suddenly had more time to dive deeper into crypto. My English had improved significantly, which helped me access better resources. I started buying Bitcoin and altcoins again. The bull run of 2021 was a game-changer—it completely transformed my life. Everything I had invested in before 2021 skyrocketed in value, with returns averaging 10x-20x.

Becoming a Crypto Influencer

As my portfolio grew, I started making videos on YouTube to share my journey. Due to the increase of demand and available time I had because of the COVID 19 lockdown in Greece, I kept doing more videos, and to my surprise, I became a crypto YouTuber, something I had never imagined. By mid-2021, I was earning an average of $80,000 monthly from my crypto investments and my growing income as an influencer. That was an immense leap from the $5,000 monthly income I had been used to.

However, with my newfound wealth came a major realization: in Greece, I would have to pay 45% of my earnings in taxes, even though there were no clear regulations for crypto. That pushed me to search for solutions. Eventually, I decided to move to Dubai (United Arab Emirates), where there are no taxes on crypto. This decision allowed me to scale my investments and businesses without the burden of high taxes.

I reinvested my profits into my growing influencer business, affiliate marketing, sponsorships, and a marketing agency. From January 2021 to November 2024, I created over 4,000 pieces of content across all my social media platforms. I became the #1 crypto content creator in Greece and Cyprus and authored two bestselling books: *The Bible of Cryptocurrency* in Greek and *The Ultimate Guide to Cryptocurrency* in English.

Challenges in 2022: The Bear Market

The year 2022 was an interesting and challenging one. The market entered a bear phase, and big crypto companies like FTX and Celsius Network collapsed. Many people became uncertain about the future of crypto, but I stayed focused. I kept accumulating assets, building my business, hiring people, and preparing for the next bull run. I knew that markets would eventually recover, and this time, I wanted to be even more prepared to take full advantage of the opportunities presented by this innovative technology.

A Turning Point: Bitcoin Mining

By January 2023, I felt the need to elevate my game. I had mastered investing and generating income across industries but wasn't a multi-millionaire or billionaire. I started studying the world's wealthiest people, understanding how major funds like BlackRock operate, and analyzing their strategies, as well as how decisions on interest rates, inflation, and money printing control various aspects of the economy. This research fueled my desire to gain more control over my financial destiny and inspired me to explore Bitcoin mining.

In May 2023, after extensive research, I launched my first Bitcoin mining operation. The moment I mined my first $100, I felt a profound sense of freedom. Over time, I scaled my mining investments, eventually founding Bitmern Mining, which provides Bitcoin mining services, hosting, management, education, and consulting. Today, Bitmern Mining manages over $2 million worth of equipment.

Scaling My Crypto Empire

In addition to mining, I've launched several businesses under the Bitmern brand:
1. Bitmern Taxes: A platform for automating crypto tax calculations.
2. Bitmern Staking: A platform for staking crypto to earn passive income.
3. Bitmern Capital: An investment fund for well-informed investors.

My portfolio now includes 89 crypto nodes across 15 projects, alongside my growing collection of Bitcoin and altcoins. I've built multiple revenue streams, reinvesting in businesses and assets to ensure long-term growth.

My Crypto Philosophy

Crypto has been more than an investment—it's a lifestyle and a mission. My guiding principles are:
1. Accumulate Bitcoin (at least 50% of my portfolio).
2. Invest in quality altcoins during bull markets, exit at the peak, and convert gains to Bitcoin and stablecoins.
3. Reinvest profits into long-term portfolio growth and business development.
4. Build scalable businesses to diversify income streams.
5. Educate others through videos, books, live events, and podcasts.

Lessons Learned

Over the past four years, I've spent thousands of hours learning and teaching about crypto. During this time, I've also had the privilege of meeting hundreds of founders and CEOs in the crypto industry. Learning from their experiences and following their advice has given me a deeper understanding of the industry and shaped my approach to success. While I'm not yet a billionaire, I've built a multi-million-dollar empire through hard work, determination, and a willingness to adapt.

Without any formal education, having dropped out of school at 15, I've accomplished what once seemed impossible. Bitcoin and crypto made this journey possible, giving me the tools to create financial freedom and inspire others to do the same. My story proves that with knowledge, persistence, innovation, and the right guidance, anyone can transform their life. The journey isn't over, and I'm excited to keep building, learning, and sharing this incredible experience with the world.

The journey has only just begun.

Part 11. Bitcoin's Potential to Secure Your Family's Financial Future

Bitcoin represents a transformative shift in how wealth can be preserved, protected, and grown. Its unique properties—decentralization, scarcity, and global accessibility—offer a powerful tool for securing your family's financial future, particularly in an era of economic uncertainty, inflation, and evolving financial systems. Here's how Bitcoin can play a pivotal role in creating financial stability and prosperity for your family.

1. How Bitcoin Can Secure Your Family's Financial Future

A. Diversification in Wealth Building

Bitcoin acts as a hedge within a diversified portfolio, complementing traditional investments like real estate, stocks, and bonds.

Its low correlation with other asset classes makes it a valuable addition, reducing overall portfolio risk while enhancing potential returns.

B. Creating Long-Term Wealth

By adopting a long-term holding strategy (HODLing), families can take advantage of Bitcoin's historical price growth.

Example: Over the past decade, Bitcoin has consistently outperformed traditional asset classes, with an annualized return exceeding 100% in its early years.

C. Supporting Education and Future Goals

Families can use Bitcoin to fund education, home purchases, or entrepreneurial ventures for future generations.

Gradual liquidation of Bitcoin holdings during times of need can provide a steady source of funding without depleting the family's overall wealth.

2. Strategies for Integrating Bitcoin into Family Wealth Planning

A. Start Small and Build Over Time

Consistently allocate a portion of family income to Bitcoin through Dollar-Cost Averaging (DCA). This strategy minimizes the impact of price volatility and builds wealth steadily over time.

B. Multi-Generational Custody Solutions

Use advanced tools like multisignature wallets to manage family-held Bitcoin. These wallets require multiple keys to access funds, ensuring that decisions about spending or transferring wealth are made collectively.

C. Leverage Bitcoin for Passive Growth

Families can earn passive income by lending Bitcoin on trusted platforms or staking wrapped Bitcoin on decentralized finance (DeFi) protocols.

These strategies allow families to grow their holdings while retaining ownership of their Bitcoin.

D. Pair Bitcoin with Traditional Assets

Develop a balanced strategy by combining Bitcoin with traditional investments such as real estate or equities. This diversification protects against short-term volatility while maintaining exposure to Bitcoin's long-term growth potential.

3. Real-World Case Studies of Bitcoin Securing Families' Future

Case Study 1: Wealth Preservation in Hyperinflationary Economies

A family in Turkey converted its savings into Bitcoin during a period of rapid lira devaluation. Over time, Bitcoin's price appreciation helped the family maintain its purchasing power and fund their children's education abroad.

Case Study 2: Cross-Border Wealth Transfer

A family from Venezuela used Bitcoin to migrate to Europe. By converting their wealth into Bitcoin and securing it in a mobile wallet, they avoided capital controls and ensured financial stability upon arrival.

Case Study 3: Multi-Generational Bitcoin Fund

A tech-savvy family in the U.S. established a Bitcoin trust, allocating a portion of their holdings for each generation. The trust is structured to release Bitcoin gradually, ensuring that wealth continues to grow while supporting future family milestones.

4. The Role of Bitcoin in Financial Independence

Breaking Free from Traditional Systems

Bitcoin allows families to bypass fees, delays, and limitations associated with traditional banking systems, enabling more efficient wealth management.

Its decentralized nature ensures that families are not reliant on government-backed systems that may fail during economic downturns.

Empowering Financial Literacy

By incorporating Bitcoin into financial planning, families foster a culture of innovation and learning. Teaching younger generations about Bitcoin equips them with the tools to navigate a rapidly digitizing economy.

5. Real-World Examples of Bitcoin in Family Wealth

A Modern-Day Dowry

In some cultures, Bitcoin is becoming a part of modern dowries, symbolizing prosperity and future security for couples.

Generational Bitcoin Vaults

Wealthy families are creating 'generational vaults' of Bitcoin, secured by advanced multi-signature wallets. These vaults are built to endure for decades, preserving the family's legacy.

Philanthropy Through Bitcoin

Bitcoin's global nature makes it an ideal tool for charitable giving. Families are setting up Bitcoin-based philanthropic funds to benefit future generations while supporting causes they care about.

6. Challenges to Consider

While Bitcoin offers unique advantages for wealth transfer, there are challenges to consider:

Volatility

Bitcoin's price fluctuations can be significant, requiring families to adopt strategies like DCA or diversification to manage risk. Families must plan for market swings.

Regulatory Uncertainty

While Bitcoin adoption is growing, regulatory frameworks differ globally. Families should stay informed about local regulations and their implications for ownership and transfer.

Tax Implications

Gifting or inheriting Bitcoin may trigger taxes, depending on jurisdiction. Professional advice is essential.

Security Risks

Ensuring the secure custody of Bitcoin is paramount. Families must use trusted wallets and follow best practices to prevent loss or theft.

Bitcoin offers families a unique opportunity to secure their financial future in an increasingly uncertain world. By adopting strategic planning, educating family members, and integrating Bitcoin into a diversified financial plan, families can ensure stability, resilience, and prosperity for future generations. Bitcoin is not just a technological innovation—it's a gateway to financial independence and a brighter future for those willing to embrace its potential.

Part 12. Bitcoin's Role in Your Financial Legacy Innovative Strategies for Multi-Generational Wealth

Building a financial legacy has long been a cornerstone of family planning, and Bitcoin is redefining how wealth is stored, preserved, and passed on to future generations. Beyond traditional methods like trusts and wills, Bitcoin offers a new dimension to legacy planning, enabling innovative strategies tailored to its unique characteristics.

In this part, we explore how families and individuals leverage Bitcoin to create and transfer enduring wealth for their descendants.

1. The Generational Wealth Revolution with Bitcoin

Bitcoin represents more than an investment; it's a paradigm shift in how wealth is perceived and managed. Unlike traditional assets, Bitcoin is:

- Borderless: Transferable across countries without intermediaries.

- Immutable: Cannot be confiscated or altered by external forces.

- Deflationary: Its finite supply ensures long-term value preservation, unlike fiat currencies subject to inflation.

Families that recognize Bitcoin's transformative potential are adopting strategies to incorporate it into their long-term wealth plans.

2. Innovative Bitcoin Legacy Strategies

A. Multi-Generational Bitcoin Trusts

- Families are creating Bitcoin-backed trusts to secure and grow wealth for future generations.
- Trusts hold Bitcoin as a long-term asset and may include provisions for:
  - Gradual disbursement to heirs based on milestones (e.g., age, education, or financial maturity).
  - Protection from potential mismanagement by younger generations.

Case Example:
A family sets up a trust with 10 Bitcoins and appoints a trustee to oversee its growth. The trust is programmed to release portions of the Bitcoin to each heir at specific intervals, ensuring they receive support throughout their lives while the core wealth continues to grow.

B. Strategic Gifting Across Generations

Families are increasingly gifting Bitcoin to their children and grandchildren as a means of wealth transfer. This strategy can take several forms:

- Early Gifting: Transferring Bitcoin while it's still relatively affordable to maximize future growth.
- Educational Gifting: Gifting small amounts of Bitcoin alongside financial education to introduce heirs to the asset's potential.

Benefits:

- Gifting Bitcoin early allows heirs to participate in its price appreciation.
- Introducing heirs to Bitcoin fosters financial literacy and responsibility.

C. Bitcoin as a Hedge for Future Generations

Bitcoin is used as a hedge against systemic risks such as hyperinflation, political instability, or economic downturns. Families in regions with unstable economies often allocate a portion of their wealth to Bitcoin to protect against local currency devaluation.

Example: In countries like Venezuela and Turkey, families have converted savings into Bitcoin to shield their wealth from hyperinflation. By doing so, they ensure that future generations inherit assets with global value.

D. Fractionalized Wealth Transfer

Unlike traditional assets, Bitcoin can be easily divided into small units (satoshis). This divisibility allows for:

- Fair Distribution: Families can allocate exact portions of Bitcoin to heirs, avoiding disputes over asset division.

- Phased Inheritance: Wealth can be transferred incrementally, ensuring heirs receive support over time rather than in a lump sum.

3. Long-Term Bitcoin Growth Strategies

A. Leveraging Bitcoin's Store of Value

Families are holding Bitcoin as a long-term reserve asset, treating it as digital gold. Over decades, this strategy allows wealth to grow as Bitcoin appreciates.

B. Yield-Generating Bitcoin Investments

Advanced strategies involve using Bitcoin to generate passive income, such as:

- Staking: Some families use Bitcoin derivatives or wrapped Bitcoin on blockchains like Ethereum to earn staking rewards. Wrapped Bitcoin on a blockchain is Bitcoin that has been converted into a type of token on other blockchain platforms, such as Ethereum, retaining the value of Bitcoin but allowing its use in different ecosystems.

- Lending: Lending Bitcoin through trusted platforms to earn interest while maintaining ownership.

4. Combining Traditional Wealth Strategies with Bitcoin

Bitcoin doesn't need to replace traditional methods of wealth preservation—it can complement them. Here's how families are blending old and new approaches:

- Bitcoin-Backed Insurance: Combining life insurance policies with Bitcoin holdings ensures that heirs benefit from both fiat stability and Bitcoin's growth potential.

- Real Estate and Bitcoin Pairing: Families diversify their portfolios by adding Bitcoin to their real estate investments, creating a balanced mix of tangible and digital assets.

Part 13. The Bitcoin Revolution: A Call to Action

The rise of Bitcoin marks one of the most significant revolutions in modern financial history. It is not just a digital currency or an investment opportunity—it's a movement for financial freedom, transparency, and empowerment. In a world increasingly dominated by centralized power, inflationary monetary policies, and economic inequality, Bitcoin serves as a beacon of hope, offering a path toward a more equitable and decentralized future.

This part is a call to action for everyone: to understand, embrace, and contribute to the Bitcoin revolution—a movement that transcends borders, political ideologies, and economic systems.

1. The Essence of the Bitcoin Revolution

Decentralization: Power to the People

Bitcoin's decentralized network puts control back into the hands of individuals. Unlike traditional financial systems, which rely on intermediaries like banks and governments, Bitcoin operates on a peer-to-peer network, enabling anyone to send, receive, and store value without third-party interference.

Transparency and Trust

In a world where trust in financial institutions is eroding, Bitcoin offers an alternative: a transparent, immutable ledger in which transactions are recorded and verified by the community.

This transparency fosters accountability and eliminates the need to place blind trust in centralized entities.

Scarcity and Value Preservation

Bitcoin's fixed supply of 21 million coins ensures that it remains immune to inflation—a stark contrast to fiat currencies, which are continuously devalued by excessive money printing.

By design, Bitcoin protects the wealth of individuals, particularly in times of economic uncertainty and hyperinflation.

2. Why Bitcoin Matters in Our Time

A Response to Broken Systems

The 2008 financial crisis exposed the vulnerabilities of the traditional banking system. Bailouts for banks, rampant money printing, and the collapse of trust inspired the creation of Bitcoin as a solution to these systemic failures.

Today, Bitcoin continues to challenge the status quo, offering an alternative to centralized control and opaque financial practices.

Empowering the Unbanked

Over 1.4 billion people worldwide lack access to basic banking services. Bitcoin provides them with an opportunity to engage in the global economy, bypassing barriers such as geographic limitations, high fees, and bureaucratic obstacles.

Freedom from Censorship

In countries with authoritarian regimes or restrictive financial policies, Bitcoin acts as a lifeline for individuals looking to safeguard their wealth and preserve their freedom.

Whether it's activists funding movements, refugees fleeing oppressive regimes, or individuals protecting their wealth during hyperinflation, Bitcoin empowers people to fight against financial oppression.

3. The Financial Freedom Movement

Bitcoin embodies the principles of financial freedom in ways that traditional systems cannot match:

1. Ownership: Bitcoin empowers individuals to have true ownership of their money. With private keys, your wealth is under your control—not a bank's or government's.

2. Borderless Transactions: Bitcoin eliminates barriers to transferring wealth across borders, making financial inclusion a reality for everyone, everywhere.

3. Resilience: Bitcoin's decentralized infrastructure makes it resistant to censorship, confiscation, and manipulation.

4. A Global Movement for Change

The Role of Individuals

Every person who buys, holds, or advocates for Bitcoin is contributing to a larger movement for financial independence and sovereignty.

By adopting Bitcoin, you're not just investing in an asset—you're supporting a vision of a world where money is fair, free, and accessible to everyone.

The Role of Communities

Local initiatives like Bitcoin Beach in El Salvador or grassroots education efforts in Nigeria demonstrate how Bitcoin can uplift entire communities.

These projects show the power of collective action in driving Bitcoin adoption and creating real-world change.

The Role of Governments and Institutions

Progressive governments and institutions are beginning to recognize Bitcoin's potential, from El Salvador adopting it as legal tender to companies like Tesla and MicroStrategy integrating it into their balance sheets.

As more entities embrace Bitcoin, its legitimacy and global influence will grow.

5. Overcoming Challenges

Education is Key

Many people remain skeptical of Bitcoin due to misinformation or lack of understanding. Education is the cornerstone of adoption and a critical step in the Bitcoin revolution.

Regulatory Clarity

Governments must establish clear and fair regulations that allow Bitcoin to thrive while protecting consumers. Advocacy for thoughtful policy-making is essential.

Adapting to Technological Advancements

The Bitcoin community must continue to innovate, ensuring scalability, energy efficiency, and usability to support mass adoption.

6. How You Can Join the Revolution

1. Start Learning:
   Educate yourself about Bitcoin's technology, benefits, and potential. Resources like books, podcasts, and online courses can help you get started.

2. Buy Bitcoin:
   Even a small investment can be a powerful step toward participating in the Bitcoin ecosystem.

3. Spread Awareness:
   Share your knowledge with others, dispel myths and encourage them to explore Bitcoin's potential.

4. Advocate for Adoption:
   Support businesses that accept Bitcoin, advocate for progressive policies, and contribute to community initiatives.

5. Secure Your Bitcoin:
   Learn about self-custody and the importance of holding your private keys to fully own your Bitcoin.

Is It Too Late to Buy Bitcoin?

One of the most common questions people ask when considering Bitcoin is: *"Is it too late to buy Bitcoin?"* The short answer is: ***"No, it is never truly too late"*** — but it depends on your perspective, time horizon, and your understanding of Bitcoin's long-term potential. Bitcoin remains an opportunity as long as its price is below $1,000,000 because of its vast **potential to reach $13,000,000 or more in the next 20 years**.

Let's break this down with historical examples, psychology, and what the future might hold.

1. Bitcoin's History: What Seemed Expensive Then is Cheap Now

It's important to remember that every Bitcoin milestone once seemed 'too high' for investors at the time. Let's look at some key moments:

- **2011**: Bitcoin hit $31 for the first time and then dropped to $2. Imagine buying at $31 and watching your investment plummet—many believed they had bought at the peak.
  But today? $31 is laughably cheap. That $31 Bitcoin has grown **thousands of times** in value.
- **2013**: Bitcoin reached $1,000. People thought, *"This is ridiculous! How could it go higher?"* Many believed they were too late.
  Fast forward 11 years later: Bitcoin has grown **over 100X**.
- **2017**: Bitcoin skyrocketed to **$16,000**. Once again, fear set in: *"Bitcoin is overpriced; it can't possibly grow further."*
  Today, looking back, most investors wish they had bought Bitcoin at $16,000.
- **2021**: Bitcoin hit an all-time high of **$69,000** before dropping significantly. People panicked and assumed it was the end. But now, Bitcoin has surpassed previous records, and those who bought at $69,000—or earlier—are sitting on high gains.
  Today, **everyone who saw Bitcoin below $100,000 wishes they had bought more.**

The lesson? Bitcoin always feels expensive at its peak, but over time, those 'high' prices look like bargains in hindsight.

2. The Future: Why Bitcoin Under $1 Million Is Still an Opportunity

Bitcoin is still in its early stages of global adoption. The growing demand, combined with its fixed supply of **21 million coins**, makes it a unique and scarce asset that probably will continue appreciating. If Bitcoin reaches **$1,000,000,** people will look back at today's prices and say, *"I wish I had bought Bitcoin when it was still under a million."*

From now on, that will be understood more by:

- Smart investors, institutions, and even governments are beginning to understand Bitcoin's value as 'digital gold.'
- Institutional adoption is accelerating, with Bitcoin ETFs, banks, and sovereign wealth funds now integrating Bitcoin into their portfolios.
- The psychology of investors will shift as Bitcoin surpasses $1 million, making sub-$1 million prices seem like the ultimate bargain.

If you're investing with a **long-term mindset**, as long as Bitcoin remains under $1,000,000, it's still a massive opportunity.

3. Psychology: Understanding the Investor's Mindset

Human psychology plays an immense role in why people hesitate to invest in Bitcoin:

1. **Fear of Volatility**:
   Bitcoin's price history is full of dramatic rises and crashes. People who bought at peaks often panic during downturns, selling their holdings instead of holding long-term. History has shown that patience pays off.

2. **The Perception of 'Too Late'**:
   Each time Bitcoin reaches a new high, it feels like the opportunity has passed. However, Bitcoin's track record shows that new highs are often followed by even higher ones in the future.

3. **Lack of Understanding**:
   Many investors, banks, and governments are still catching up to Bitcoin's potential. As understanding grows, demand will increase, driving prices even higher.

4. What Does This Mean for You?

If you are a long-term investor, the answer is clear: **It's not too late to buy Bitcoin.**

Bitcoin's upward trajectory over the last 15 years demonstrates that temporary dips and volatility are part of its natural growth.

Whether you buy at $30,000, $100,000, or even $500,000, the real question is: *Where will Bitcoin be in 10, 15, or 20 years?*

Many experts and investors believe Bitcoin has the potential to reach **$1,000,000**, **$5,000,000**, or even **$13,000,000** in the coming decades. At that point, today's prices will look like an unimaginable bargain.

The decision is ultimately yours. Bitcoin's limited supply, increasing demand, and revolutionary nature make it a unique asset in history. The sooner you take action, the greater your opportunity to be a part of this financial revolution.

Imagine the future: **Would you regret not buying Bitcoin under $1 million?** For most people, the answer is yes. If history repeats itself—and it often does—there will come a time when today's prices look like a missed opportunity.

The choice is simple:
Take action now, or watch from the sidelines. The Bitcoin revolution waits for no one.

7. The Call to Action

The Bitcoin revolution isn't just about money—it's about freedom, empowerment, and a more equitable world. It's a chance to take control of your financial future, challenge the status quo, and contribute to a movement that transcends borders, ideologies, and generations.

This is your moment to be part of something historic. Whether you're an investor, an advocate, or simply curious, your participation matters. Together, we can build a future where financial freedom isn't a privilege but a universal right.

Bitcoin is more than a technological innovation; it's a revolution that empowers individuals, disrupts broken systems, and redefines the concept of money. This revolution invites you to participate, not just as a spectator, but as an active force in shaping the future of finance.

Will you answer the call?

Part 14. The Philosophy of Bitcoin: Beyond Money

Bitcoin is commonly referred to as digital money or a store of value, but its essence extends far beyond these definitions. At its core, Bitcoin represents a profound philosophical shift—a movement for freedom, privacy, and decentralization. It challenges the traditional structures of power and control, offering an alternative vision of how society can interact with money, technology, and authority.

This part explores Bitcoin as a transformative idea, examining its philosophical foundations and role in shaping a more equitable and decentralized future.

1. Freedom: The Foundation of Bitcoin's Philosophy

Financial Sovereignty

Bitcoin empowers individuals to take control of their wealth without relying on intermediaries like banks or governments. By owning private keys, users have direct access to their funds, free from external control or interference.

In a world where financial systems can be manipulated, censored, or weaponized, Bitcoin provides a lifeline for those seeking autonomy over their financial destiny.

Breaking Barriers

Traditional financial systems exclude billions of people due to geographic, political, or economic barriers. Bitcoin's borderless nature ensures that anyone with an internet connection can participate in the global economy, fostering financial inclusion.

A New Paradigm

Bitcoin shifts the balance of power from centralized institutions to individuals. It challenges the monopoly of central banks on money creation and empowers people to transact freely, regardless of borders or governments.

2. Privacy: Protecting Individual Rights in the Digital Age

The Erosion of Privacy

In today's digital world, financial transactions are frequently monitored, tracked, and recorded by governments and corporations. This constant surveillance erodes privacy and can lead to discrimination, censorship, or abuse of power.

Bitcoin as a Shield

Bitcoin offers financial privacy, enabling peer-to-peer transactions without requiring personal information. While the Bitcoin blockchain is transparent, users can protect their identities through careful practices like generating new addresses for each transaction.

A Step Toward Anonymity

Innovations like the Lightning Network and privacy-enhancing tools (e.g., CoinJoin) continue to improve Bitcoin's ability to protect user identities. These advancements align with Bitcoin's ethos of empowering individuals to operate freely in the digital economy.

3. Decentralization: Challenging Centralized Control

The Problem with Centralization

Centralized systems are vulnerable to corruption, inefficiency, and single points of failure. Whether it's a banking collapse, government overreach, or a data breach, reliance on centralized entities often puts individuals at risk.

Bitcoin's Decentralized Solution

Bitcoin's network is supported by thousands of nodes distributed worldwide. This decentralization ensures that no single entity can control or shut down the system.

The consensus mechanism, proof of work, ensures that decisions about Bitcoin's future are made collectively, not dictated by a central authority.

Empowering Communities

Decentralization isn't just about technology; it's about fostering communities where power is distributed and everyone has a voice. Bitcoin's open-source nature allows anyone to contribute to its development, creating a truly democratic financial system.

4. The Philosophy of 'Code is Law'

Immutable Rules

Bitcoin's protocol is governed by unchangeable rules, not the whims of politicians or central bankers. These rules, such as the 21 million coin cap, create predictability and trust in a system without human intervention.

This concept—referred to as 'code is law'—marks a significant departure from traditional systems, where rules can be changed to serve specific interests.

Trustless Transactions

Bitcoin eliminates the need for trust between parties by replacing it with cryptographic proof. This trustless nature ensures fairness and security, enabling global commerce without intermediaries.

5. Bitcoin as a Movement

A Rebellion Against Financial Oppression

For people in authoritarian regimes, Bitcoin offers a means to resist censorship and control. It enables dissidents to fund movements, refugees to preserve wealth, and citizens to bypass oppressive capital controls.

A New Form of Activism

Bitcoin advocates often see themselves as part of a larger movement to decentralize power and promote individual freedom. This activism goes beyond technology, encompassing education, advocacy, and grassroots initiatives like Bitcoin Beach in El Salvador.

A Global Community

Bitcoin has united millions of people worldwide who share a common belief in its transformative potential. From developers and miners to investors and educators, the Bitcoin community is diverse but united by a shared philosophy.

Balancing Privacy and Transparency

Bitcoin's open ledger maintains a balance between transparency and privacy, but some question whether it can truly protect user identities. Future developments must address these concerns while maintaining decentralization.

Inspiring Future Innovations

Bitcoin's principles have inspired countless projects and innovations, from decentralized finance (DeFi) to decentralized autonomous organizations (DAOs). These advancements build on Bitcoin's foundation, expanding its impact on the world.

Bitcoin's true value lies not in its price but in its philosophy. It challenges the status quo, presents a vision of financial sovereignty, and sparks a movement that transcends borders and ideologies. Bitcoin is more than a currency—it's a statement about the kind of world we want to create: one that values freedom, privacy, and decentralization.

By understanding and embracing Bitcoin's philosophy, we take a step toward building a more equitable and empowered future. The revolution begins with you.

Part 15. Bitcoin and the Global South: Transforming Economies in Developing Nations

1. The Economic Challenges of the Global South

A. Limited Access to Banking

Over 1.4 billion adults worldwide remain unbanked, with a disproportionate number living in developing nations. These individuals lack access to basic financial services like savings accounts, credit, and payment systems.

Reasons include:
- High banking fees.
- Geographic inaccessibility.
- Distrust of traditional financial institutions.

B. Remittance Dependence

Remittances from abroad are a significant source of income in many countries in the Global South, but traditional methods like Western Union charge exorbitant fees and can take days to process.

2. Bitcoin as a Solution for the Global South

A. Financial Inclusion

Bitcoin allows individuals to bypass traditional banking systems, providing access to financial services with a smartphone and an internet connection.

Peer-to-peer (P2P) platforms like Paxful and Binance P2P enable people to trade Bitcoin directly, avoiding high banking fees.

B. A Hedge Against Inflation

Bitcoin's fixed supply of 21 million coins makes it immune to inflation, offering a reliable store of value for individuals in unstable economies.

C. Low-Cost Remittances

Bitcoin allows migrant workers to send money home instantly and at a fraction of the cost of traditional remittance services.

Platforms like Strike and Bitcoin Beach Wallet facilitate cross-border transactions using Bitcoin or the Lightning Network, making remittances faster and cheaper.

D. Empowering Entrepreneurs

Bitcoin enables small business owners to accept global payments without relying on expensive intermediaries.

Examples include artisans selling goods online and farmers using Bitcoin to trade directly with international buyers.

3. Real-World Examples of Bitcoin Transforming Economies

A. El Salvador: Bitcoin as Legal Tender

In 2021, El Salvador became the first country to adopt Bitcoin as legal tender, alongside the U.S. dollar.

Impact:
- Citizens use Bitcoin for everyday transactions via government-issued wallets like Chivo Wallet.
- The country has attracted international attention and investment as a Bitcoin hub.
- Communities like Bitcoin Beach showcase how Bitcoin can drive financial inclusion and economic development.

B. Nigeria: A Hub for Bitcoin Adoption

Nigeria has emerged as a global leader in Bitcoin adoption, with more than 32% of Nigerians using cryptocurrencies.

Why Bitcoin Matters in Nigeria:

- Strict capital controls limit access to foreign currency.
- High inflation drives citizens to seek alternative stores of value.
- Bitcoin is used for remittances, payments, and savings, bypassing traditional banking constraints.

C. Venezuela: Surviving Hyperinflation

Amid hyperinflation, Venezuelans have turned to Bitcoin as a stable alternative to the bolívar.

- P2P trading platforms like LocalBitcoins have flourished, enabling citizens to buy essentials like food and medicine with Bitcoin.
- Businesses accept Bitcoin to preserve value and access international markets.

D. Zimbabwe: A Currency Alternative

In Zimbabwe, Bitcoin is an alternative to the Zimbabwean dollar, which has experienced repeated devaluations.

Citizens use Bitcoin to store savings and transact with more stability than the national currency offers.

4. Broader Impacts of Bitcoin on Developing Economies

A. Stimulating Local Economies

Bitcoin adoption encourages local entrepreneurship, job creation, and innovation.

Example: Communities like Bitcoin Beach in El Salvador and Bitcoin Ekasi in South Africa use Bitcoin to fund local projects and create economic opportunities.

B. Fostering Financial Independence

By eliminating intermediaries, Bitcoin empowers individuals to take control of their finances, reducing dependency on unstable governments and corrupt financial institutions.

C. Driving Technological Literacy

As Bitcoin adoption grows, so does interest in blockchain technology, coding, and digital entrepreneurship. That creates opportunities for education and skills development in underserved regions.

5. Challenges and Critiques

A. Volatility
Bitcoin's price fluctuations can pose risks for individuals relying on it as a stable store of value or medium of exchange.

B. Lack of Infrastructure
Limited internet access and technological infrastructure in some regions hinder Bitcoin adoption.

C. Education and Awareness
Many individuals in developing nations lack the knowledge or confidence to adopt Bitcoin, highlighting the need for educational initiatives.

6. The Future of Bitcoin in the Global South

A. Expanding Adoption

As Bitcoin becomes more accessible through mobile apps, P2P platforms, and educational efforts, its adoption is expected to grow exponentially in the Global South.

B. Innovative Solutions

Projects like the Lightning Network are making Bitcoin transactions faster and cheaper, increasing its utility for everyday use in developing economies.

C. Collaboration and Investment

Partnerships between governments, NGOs (Non-Governmental Organizations), and private companies can further drive Bitcoin adoption and its integration into local economies.

Bitcoin is not just a tool for wealth preservation in the Global South—it's a catalyst for transformation. By addressing critical challenges like inflation, banking exclusion, and remittance inefficiencies, Bitcoin empowers individuals, revitalizes communities, and reshapes economies.

As Bitcoin adoption continues to grow in developing nations, it demonstrates its potential to level the financial playing field, offering opportunities for prosperity and independence to millions of people. The Bitcoin revolution is not just a global phenomenon—it's a lifeline for the Global South, where its impact is felt most profoundly.

Part 16. Stories of Individuals in Hyperinflationary Environments Using Bitcoin to Survive

In countries grappling with hyperinflation, where local currencies lose value daily, Bitcoin has emerged as a lifeline for countless individuals. By offering an alternative to rapidly devaluing fiat currencies, Bitcoin enables people to preserve their wealth, access essential goods and services, and navigate economic turmoil. Here are compelling stories of how Bitcoin has helped individuals survive and thrive in hyperinflationary environments like Venezuela and Zimbabwe.

1. Maria's Story: A Teacher's Lifeline in Venezuela

In Venezuela, hyperinflation has rendered the bolívar worthless, leaving citizens struggling to afford necessities. Maria, a middle-school teacher in Caracas, saw her salary diminish to just a few U.S. dollars per month. Desperate for a solution, Maria turned to Bitcoin.

How Bitcoin Helped:
- Maria began accepting payments for tutoring in Bitcoin, using platforms like LocalBitcoins to trade BTC for goods and services.
- She used Bitcoin to buy groceries and medicine from international vendors, bypassing the collapsing local economy.
- By saving in Bitcoin instead of bolívars, Maria preserved her earnings, shielding herself from hyperinflation's devastating effects.

Outcome:
Today, Maria credits Bitcoin not only with helping her survive but also with giving her hope for a more secure financial future.

2. Carlos and Ana: Entrepreneurs Thriving with Bitcoin

Carlos and Ana owned a small bakery in Maracaibo, Venezuela, which struggled to stay afloat as the bolívar's value plummeted. Inflation made it impossible to predict costs or set stable prices, so the couple decided to adopt Bitcoin as part of their business strategy.

How Bitcoin Helped:
- They began accepting Bitcoin as payment, attracting tech-savvy customers who preferred digital transactions.
- With Bitcoin, they could import baking supplies from abroad, avoiding inflated local prices and unreliable payment systems.
- By reinvesting profits into Bitcoin, they protected their savings from further devaluation.

Outcome:
The bakery not only survived but expanded, becoming one of the first businesses in their city to thrive amidst the economic chaos.

3. Samuel's Story: Resilience in Zimbabwe

Samuel, a university student in Harare, Zimbabwe, witnessed hyperinflation erase his family's life savings. The collapse of the Zimbabwean dollar left them unable to afford tuition or purchase essentials. Seeking a way to secure his future, Samuel discovered Bitcoin through friends.

How Bitcoin Helped:
- Samuel began mining Bitcoin using a laptop and a small solar panel, taking advantage of Zimbabwe's abundant sunlight.
- He used Bitcoin to pay for his education and support his family by trading it for U.S. dollars on peer-to-peer platforms.
- Bitcoin enabled him to bypass the Zimbabwean banking system, plagued by currency shortages and transaction limits.

Outcome:
Samuel graduated debt-free and now teaches others in his community about Bitcoin's potential to overcome economic instability.

4. Rosa's Story: Feeding Her Family with Bitcoin

Rosa, a single mother of three in Venezuela, faced heartbreaking choices as rampant inflation made it impossible to afford food for her children. Expensive and unreliable traditional remittance services, such as Western Union, only compounded her struggles.

How Bitcoin Helped:
- Rosa's brother, living in the United States, began sending her remittances in Bitcoin. She used a smartphone app to receive the funds instantly.
- By converting small amounts of Bitcoin into bolívars as needed, Rosa avoided the rapid devaluation of her local currency.
- Bitcoin's low fees and speed allowed her to stretch every dollar further, ensuring her children could eat.

Outcome:
Bitcoin became Rosa's financial lifeline, providing stability and a sense of control in the midst of economic chaos.

5. Tariro's Story: Empowering Women in Zimbabwe

In Zimbabwe, where financial independence for women is often limited, Tariro, a seamstress, faced unique challenges. She struggled to save money as hyperinflation rapidly rendered her earnings worthless.

How Bitcoin Helped:
- Tariro joined a women's cooperative that introduced her to Bitcoin. She began saving her profits in BTC, avoiding the devaluation of the Zimbabwean dollar.
- She used Bitcoin to purchase sewing supplies from international vendors and to receive payments from customers abroad.
- Bitcoin's borderless nature allowed her to expand her business beyond Zimbabwe's economic restrictions.

Outcome:
Tariro gained financial independence and now mentors other women on using Bitcoin to secure their futures.

6. The Story of Bitcoin Communities

In addition to individual stories, entire communities in hyperinflationary environments have adopted Bitcoin as a means of survival and empowerment.

- Bitcoin Ekasi (South Africa):
    - A township community in South Africa adopted Bitcoin to create a circular economy, where residents transact exclusively in BTC.
    - This initiative has helped shield the community from the economic challenges of the region while fostering financial literacy.
- Bitcoin Beach (El Salvador):
  Before Bitcoin became legal tender, Bitcoin Beach showcased how a grassroots initiative could empower an entire community to use Bitcoin for daily transactions, education, and economic development.

7. Lessons from Their Stories

These individuals and communities demonstrate the power of Bitcoin to:

- Preserve Wealth: Bitcoin's scarcity and resistance to inflation provide a stable alternative to collapsing fiat currencies.
- Enable Access: Bitcoin's decentralized and borderless nature ensures that anyone, anywhere, can participate in the global economy.
- Foster Independence: By bypassing traditional systems, Bitcoin empowers people to take control of their financial futures.

In hyperinflationary environments, Bitcoin is not just an investment—it's a tool for survival and hope. From preserving savings to enabling commerce and fostering independence, Bitcoin has transformed the lives of individuals like Maria, Carlos, Samuel, Rosa, and Tariro. Their stories testify to Bitcoin's potential to foster resilience and create opportunities amid economic adversity.

As Bitcoin adoption grows, its ability to uplift those in the most challenging circumstances will only strengthen, proving that it is far more than a digital asset—it's a lifeline for those who need it most.

Part 17. Decoding the Psychology of Bitcoin Investors

Bitcoin has captured the imagination of millions around the world, but its appeal goes beyond its price movements or technological innovations. At its core, Bitcoin's ascent is driven by the distinct psychology of its investors—people who see it as more than just an asset. From early adopters to long-term holders (HODLers) and those swept up in the Fear of Missing Out (FOMO) phenomenon, understanding the motivations and mindsets of these groups provides valuable insights into the driving forces behind Bitcoin's adoption and market behavior.

1. Early Adopters: The Visionaries

Who Are They?

Early adopters are the pioneers who believed in Bitcoin before it had any significant value or widespread recognition. They recognized the potential of a decentralized currency long before it caught the attention of the mainstream world.

Mindset and Motivation

- Belief in the Technology:
  Early adopters often possessed a deep understanding of blockchain and its potential to revolutionize monetary systems and power structures. Many were cypherpunks, technologists, or libertarians who viewed Bitcoin as a tool for financial freedom and privacy.

- Risk Tolerance:
  Investing in Bitcoin during its infancy required a willingness to take on extreme risk, as it was unproven and volatile.

- Ideological Commitment:
  Early adopters were driven by a belief in decentralization and a desire to challenge the traditional financial system.

Psychological Traits

- Curiosity: A drive to explore uncharted territories of technology and finance.
- Resilience: An ability to withstand skepticism, ridicule, and financial losses during Bitcoin's early, turbulent years.
- Visionary Thinking: A capacity to see the long-term potential of a disruptive technology.

2. Long-Term Holders (HODLers): The True Believers

Who Are They?

HODLers are investors who choose to hold Bitcoin through market ups and downs, often accumulating more over time.

Mindset and Motivation

- Faith in Bitcoin's Future:
  HODLers believe Bitcoin's value will continue to rise over the long term due to its scarcity, utility, and increasing adoption.

- Indifference to Short-Term Volatility:
  HODLers focus on the big picture, ignoring day-to-day price fluctuations and market noise.

- Store of Value Mentality:
  Many HODLers view Bitcoin as 'digital gold,' a hedge against inflation, and a safe haven in uncertain times.

Psychological Traits

- Patience: A willingness to wait for years, or even decades, to realize the full potential of their investment.
- Emotional Discipline: The ability to remain calm during market crashes and resist the urge to sell during bull markets.
- Conviction: A strong belief in Bitcoin's value proposition, often reinforced by continuous learning and research.

The Role of Community

HODLers often find support and validation in Bitcoin communities, forums, and social media groups, where shared experiences strengthen their resolve.

3. The FOMO Phenomenon: The Fear of Missing Out

What is FOMO?

FOMO, or the Fear of Missing Out, is a psychological phenomenon where individuals feel compelled to act quickly, often irrationally, to avoid missing out on a potentially lucrative opportunity. In the context of Bitcoin, FOMO manifests during periods of rapid price growth or widespread media coverage.

How FOMO Affects Investors

- Impulsive Buying:
  Investors driven by FOMO often buy Bitcoin at market peaks, fearing they will miss further price increases. That can lead to over-leveraged positions and emotional decision-making.

- Overestimation of Potential Gains:
  FOMO can cause people to ignore risks, focusing solely on the possibility of massive returns.

- Social Validation:
  Seeing friends, family, or influencers profit from Bitcoin can trigger FOMO, pushing individuals to enter the market without adequate research.

Psychological Traits

- Emotional Reactivity: Acting on emotions rather than logic, often influenced by hype.
- Short-Term Focus: FOMO investors typically lack a long-term perspective, prioritizing immediate gains.
- Regret Aversion: Fear of future regret drives impulsive decisions, as individuals want to avoid missing a significant opportunity.

4. Behavioral Patterns in Bitcoin Investors

The FOMO Cycle

FOMO often leads to herd behavior, amplifying Bitcoin's price volatility:

1. Media Hype: Positive news or price surges attract new investors.
2. Buying Frenzy: FOMO-driven investors rush to buy Bitcoin, driving prices higher.
3. Market Correction: As prices stabilize or fall, FOMO investors panic-sell, often at a loss.

The Diamond Hands vs. Paper Hands Debate

- Diamond Hands: Investors who hold onto Bitcoin regardless of market conditions, demonstrating unwavering confidence.
- Paper Hands: Investors who sell at the first sign of trouble, often miss out on long-term gains.

5. Lessons from Bitcoin Investor Psychology

Embracing Volatility

Successful Bitcoin investors view volatility not as a threat but as an opportunity. HODLers use market dips to accumulate more, while traders capitalize on price swings.

Understanding FOMO

Recognizing the signs of FOMO can help investors avoid impulsive decisions.

Take time to research and understand Bitcoin before investing.

Develop a clear investment strategy, such as Dollar-Cost Averaging (DCA), to mitigate the effects of market emotions.

The Importance of Education

The most successful investors—whether HODLers or traders—take the time to understand Bitcoin's fundamentals, reducing the influence of fear and uncertainty.

The psychology of Bitcoin investors reveals the diverse motivations and mindsets that drive the cryptocurrency market. From the visionary early adopters who laid the groundwork for Bitcoin's rise, to the steadfast HODLers and those swayed by FOMO, each group plays a vital role in Bitcoin's journey.

Understanding these psychological dynamics can help new and experienced investors make informed decisions and align their strategies with their goals. Whether you're here for the technology, the ideology, or the profits, Bitcoin offers a space for everyone—but success lies in understanding your mindset and staying true to your vision.

Part 18. Behavioral Finance Insights: Why People Buy, Sell, or Fear Bitcoin

Bitcoin, both as a technological innovation and an emerging asset class, evokes a range of emotions and influences decision-making behaviors. Behavioral finance—a field that examines how psychological influences and biases affect financial decisions—provides valuable insights into why people buy, sell, or fear Bitcoin. Understanding these behaviors is crucial for making informed decisions and navigating the volatile world of cryptocurrency.

1. Why People Buy Bitcoin

A. Fear of Missing Out (FOMO)

- Description: Many investors are drawn to Bitcoin during bull markets when media coverage and social hype peak.

- Behavior:
  - They buy Bitcoin impulsively, fearing they'll miss the next price surge.
  - Often, these purchases occur near market peaks, leading to over-leveraged positions or buyer's remorse.

- Psychological Drivers:
  - Regret aversion: The fear of regretting missed opportunities compels action.
  - Social validation: Seeing others profit motivates people to join the trend.

B. Belief in Bitcoin's Potential

- Description: Long-term investors (HODLers) buy Bitcoin because they believe in its value as digital gold, a store of value, or a hedge against inflation.
- Behavior:
  - These buyers often adopt Dollar-Cost Averaging (DCA), consistently purchasing Bitcoin regardless of price fluctuations.
- Psychological Drivers:
  - Optimism bias: A belief that Bitcoin's price will continue to rise over the long term.
  - Confirmation bias: Seeking out information that supports their positive view of Bitcoin.

C. Diversification

- Description: Investors looking to diversify their portfolios add Bitcoin as an uncorrelated asset.
- Behavior:
  - They buy Bitcoin to reduce overall portfolio risk and enhance returns.
- Psychological Drivers:
  - Risk awareness: Acknowledging the need for alternative assets in uncertain economic conditions.
  - Herd mentality: Following the lead of institutional investors or financial advisors who recommend Bitcoin.

D. Financial Empowerment

- Description: For individuals in regions with unstable currencies or limited banking access, Bitcoin is a lifeline.
- Behavior:
  - They buy Bitcoin as a hedge against hyperinflation or a means to participate in the global economy.
- Psychological Drivers:
  - Loss aversion: A desire to avoid the devaluation of local currency.
  - Autonomy: A need for financial independence from corrupt or restrictive systems.

2. Why People Sell Bitcoin

A. Panic Selling During Downturns
- Description: Many investors sell Bitcoin when prices fall sharply, fearing additional losses.
- Behavior:
  - Panic selling often leads to locking in losses instead of waiting for a potential recovery.
- Psychological Drivers:
  - Loss aversion: The emotional pain of losing money outweighs the potential for long-term gains.
  - Anchoring bias: Fixating on the highest price Bitcoin reached and comparing current prices to that benchmark.

B. Profit-Taking
- Description: Some investors sell Bitcoin after significant price increases to realize profits.
- Behavior:
  - Profit-takers often exit too early, missing out on further upside potential.
- Psychological Drivers:
  - Sunk cost fallacy: A focus on recouping initial investments rather than evaluating future growth.
  - Immediate gratification: The urge to enjoy profits now rather than waiting for potentially higher returns.

C. Uncertainty About Bitcoin's Future
- Description: Skeptics or short-term investors sell due to regulatory fears, market volatility, or negative news.
- Behavior:
  - Selling in reaction to bad news or perceived threats, even if long-term fundamentals remain strong.
- Psychological Drivers:
  - Availability bias: Overestimating the importance of recent negative news.
  - Risk aversion: A preference for safer investments during uncertain times.

3. Why People Fear Bitcoin

A. Volatility
- Description: Bitcoin's price can experience dramatic fluctuations in short periods, creating uncertainty for investors.
- Psychological Drivers:
  - Emotional reactivity: Rapid price swings trigger fear and hesitation.
  - Conservatism bias: Preferring stable, traditional assets over high-risk alternatives.

B. Lack of Understanding
- Description: Many people fear Bitcoin because they don't fully understand how it works or its potential.
- Psychological Drivers:
  - Ambiguity aversion: Fear of the unknown discourages exploration or investment.
  - Status quo bias: A preference for familiar systems like fiat currencies or traditional investments.

C. Negative Media Coverage
- Description: Stories about scams, hacks, or regulatory crackdowns often amplify fears.
- Psychological Drivers:
  - Availability heuristic: Relying on vivid, negative stories to form judgments.
  - Groupthink: Adopting other people's fear rather than forming independent opinions.

D. Regulatory Uncertainty
- Description: Concerns about potential government bans or heavy regulations deter some investors.
- Psychological Drivers:
  - Fear of loss: Worrying about confiscation or restricted access to Bitcoin holdings.
  - Overconfidence in traditional systems: Believing that regulation will render Bitcoin ineffective or obsolete.

4. Behavioral Patterns and Lessons

Emotional Decision-Making

Emotional responses like fear, greed, and FOMO often drive impulsive decisions.

Lesson: Developing a clear strategy and focusing on long-term goals can help mitigate emotional reactions.

Herd Mentality

Following the crowd during bull or bear markets can lead to poor timing and losses.

Lesson: Independent research and critical thinking are essential for informed decision-making.

Confirmation Bias

Seeking information that aligns with preexisting beliefs can reinforce risky behaviors or missed opportunities.

Lesson: Consider diverse perspectives to form a balanced view of Bitcoin's potential.

The behavioral finance insights behind why people buy, sell, or fear Bitcoin reveal the complexity of human decision-making in the face of a revolutionary asset. Understanding these psychological drivers can help investors avoid common pitfalls, make informed choices, and align their actions with financial goals.

Bitcoin is as much about mindset as it is about technology or markets. By recognizing and managing the emotions and biases that influence behavior, investors can navigate Bitcoin's volatility with greater confidence and clarity, turning challenges into opportunities.

Part 19. Bitcoin's Impact on the Banking Industry

Bitcoin's rise as a decentralized, digital form of money fundamentally challenges the traditional banking model. As more people and institutions adopt Bitcoin, the banking industry faces a dual reality: adapt to incorporate Bitcoin into their services or risk becoming obsolete. This part explores the growing trend of Bitcoin banks and custody services, examining how Bitcoin is disrupting traditional banking systems.

1. The Rise of Bitcoin Banks and Custody Services

A. The Evolution of Bitcoin Banking

Bitcoin banks are emerging as institutions that bridge the gap between traditional banking services and the cryptocurrency ecosystem. These institutions offer:

- Custody Solutions: Safeguarding private keys for individuals and businesses.
- Crypto-Backed Loans: Allowing users to leverage their Bitcoin holdings as collateral.
- Seamless Integration: Combining fiat and Bitcoin services for users to manage both assets in one platform.

B. Major Players in Bitcoin Banking

- Companies like Coinbase, Gemini, and Kraken have introduced custody services that cater to institutional and retail clients.
- Fidelity Digital Assets and Bakkt focus on providing secure Bitcoin custody for large-scale investors, signaling growing trust in the ecosystem.
- Emerging players like Nexo offer crypto-based savings accounts and lending services, bringing traditional financial concepts into the Bitcoin world.

C. The Role of Custody Services

Custody services address a critical pain point for Bitcoin users: securing private keys.

- For individuals, custody services offer peace of mind against loss or theft.

- For institutions, they provide regulatory-compliant solutions that simplify the integration of Bitcoin into portfolios.

2. How Bitcoin Disrupts the Traditional Banking Model

A. Disintermediation of Financial Services

Bitcoin enables peer-to-peer transactions, removing the need for intermediaries like banks.

This disintermediation reduces fees, speeds up transactions, and eliminates geographic restrictions.

Example: Cross-border remittances using Bitcoin are faster and cheaper than traditional bank wires.

B. A New Paradigm for Savings and Lending

Traditional banks operate on a fractional reserve banking system, where they lend out customer deposits to generate profit. Bitcoin challenges this model:

- Bitcoin's decentralized nature allows individuals to control their assets without relying on banks.

- Crypto lending platforms like Aave and Compound enable direct lending and borrowing without intermediaries, providing transparency and higher returns.

C. Disruption of Cross-Border Transactions

Traditional banking systems are often slow and costly for international transfers due to the involvement of multiple intermediaries.

Bitcoin transactions settle within minutes, bypassing banks and reducing costs significantly.

This efficiency poses a direct challenge to SWIFT and other legacy payment networks.

D. Alternative to Inflationary Banking Systems

Banks and central banks often work together to manage economies through inflationary monetary policies, which erode the value of savings over time.

Bitcoin's fixed supply offers an alternative store of value that resists inflation, appealing to those disillusioned with fiat currency systems.

3. Challenges for Traditional Banks

A. Competition from Decentralized Finance (DeFi)

DeFi platforms provide services traditionally offered by banks, such as lending, borrowing, and earning interest, without centralized control.

These platforms often offer higher yields and greater transparency, attracting users away from traditional banks.

B. Adoption Barriers

While some banks are integrating Bitcoin services, many remain cautious due to regulatory uncertainty and perceived risks.

Resistance to change and reliance on legacy infrastructure hinder banks' ability to compete with crypto-native solutions.

C. Loss of Control

Bitcoin's decentralized nature challenges banks' monopoly on money creation and distribution.

As more people adopt Bitcoin, banks may lose their influence over monetary policies and the flow of capital.

4. The Banking Industry's Response to Bitcoin

A. Integrating Bitcoin Services

Some banks are embracing Bitcoin by offering:
- Bitcoin trading and custody for their clients.
- Bitcoin ETFs and investment products to capitalize on demand.
- Partnerships with crypto firms to expand their offerings.

Example: Banks like Standard Chartered and JP Morgan have begun integrating Bitcoin-related services, recognizing its growing importance.

B. Lobbying for Regulation

Traditional banks often lobby for stricter cryptocurrency regulations to slow Bitcoin's disruption and maintain dominance.

Some argue for frameworks that position Bitcoin as a speculative asset rather than a currency, limiting its adoption.

C. Exploring Blockchain Technology

Banks are adopting blockchain—the technology underpinning Bitcoin—to improve their operations.

Private blockchains are being developed to enable faster settlements, improve record-keeping, and enhance fraud prevention.

While not decentralized, these systems highlight the influence of Bitcoin's innovation on the banking sector.

5. The Future of Bitcoin and Banking

A. Coexistence or Displacement?

Bitcoin and traditional banks may coexist, with banks integrating Bitcoin services to stay relevant.

Alternatively, as decentralized finance and Bitcoin adoption continue to grow, traditional banks may face significant displacement.

B. A Shift in Power

Bitcoin empowers individuals by giving them direct control over their wealth, challenging the centralized authority of banks.

This democratization of finance could lead to a new era where traditional banking plays a secondary role.

C. Institutional Bitcoin Banks

The rise of institutions offering Bitcoin-specific services suggests a hybrid future where new financial entities blend traditional banking practices with decentralized principles.

Bitcoin's impact on the banking industry is profound and multifaceted. By enabling decentralized transactions, challenging traditional models, and inspiring new financial solutions, Bitcoin has forced banks to evolve or risk obsolescence.

As the lines blur between traditional and crypto finance, the future may see a world where banks act more like custodians and facilitators in a Bitcoin-dominated financial ecosystem. The revolution is ongoing, and its outcome will redefine the very foundations of banking.

Part 20. The Rise of Bitcoin in the Metaverse

As the metaverse—a convergence of virtual and augmented realities—takes shape, Bitcoin is poised to play a transformative role in these digital worlds. The metaverse envisions fully immersive, interconnected virtual environments where individuals can work, socialize, and engage in commerce. At the heart of this revolution lies the question of value and ownership, and Bitcoin, with its decentralized and secure framework, is emerging as a key player. This part explores Bitcoin's integration into the metaverse and its potential to redefine digital economies, ownership, and commerce.

1. Bitcoin's Integration into Virtual Worlds

A. The Need for Decentralized Currency in the Metaverse

Virtual economies are growing rapidly, with people spending real money on virtual goods, services, and experiences.

Bitcoin provides a universal, decentralized currency that eliminates the need for multiple in-game currencies or reliance on centralized payment processors.

Example: Bitcoin allows seamless transactions across different virtual platforms without the risk of censorship or fraud.

B. Early Integration of Bitcoin

Platforms like Decentraland and Somnium Space already support Bitcoin transactions, enabling users to buy virtual land, avatars, and digital assets.

Bitcoin's adoption in metaverse environments paves the way for a unified digital economy, offering interoperability and trust.

C. Peer-to-Peer Transactions

Bitcoin enables peer-to-peer transactions within the metaverse, allowing users to exchange value directly without intermediaries.

This aligns with the decentralized ethos of the metaverse, where control is distributed among participants.

2. Bitcoin's Role in Digital Economies

A. A Universal Store of Value

Bitcoin's scarcity and decentralization make it a reliable store of value, even in digital economies.

As virtual worlds evolve, Bitcoin can act as the backbone of financial systems, providing stability amidst the volatility of metaverse tokens.

B. Enabling Cross-Platform Commerce

In traditional gaming and virtual platforms, assets and currencies are often locked within a specific ecosystem.

Bitcoin transcends these barriers, allowing users to trade and monetize digital assets across platforms.

Example: A player could earn Bitcoin in one virtual world and spend it in another, fostering interconnected economies.

C. Powering Microtransactions

Bitcoin's divisibility allows for microtransactions—payments as small as a fraction of a cent—making it ideal for purchasing virtual items or services.

This feature is particularly valuable in metaverse economies, where users frequently transact small amounts for digital goods.

3. Transforming Ownership with Blockchain Technology

A. Decentralized Ownership

The blockchain ensures that digital assets in the metaverse—whether virtual land, artwork, or items—are securely owned and verifiable.

Bitcoin's blockchain principles inspire metaverse projects to adopt similar decentralized ownership models, preventing fraud and ensuring transparency.

B. Smart Contracts and Programmable Commerce

While Bitcoin does not natively support complex smart contracts, it can integrate with platforms like Rootstock (RSK) to enable programmable transactions.

These smart contracts facilitate automated payments, leasing of virtual properties, and royalties for creators in the metaverse.

C. NFT Integration

Non-fungible tokens (NFTs) represent unique digital assets on the blockchain. Bitcoin's Lightning Network and Layer 2 solutions enable NFT purchases and trades with low fees and high security.

Example: A virtual artist could sell their work as an NFT, accepting Bitcoin as payment while ensuring ownership through the blockchain.

D. Regulation

As virtual economies grow, governments may seek to regulate Bitcoin transactions in the metaverse, potentially impacting its adoption and usage.

E. Bridging Physical and Virtual Economies

Bitcoin creates opportunities to connect physical and digital economies, allowing users to spend virtual earnings in the real world or invest real-world assets into virtual ventures.

Bitcoin's integration with the metaverse inspires new business models, from virtual real estate markets to decentralized marketplaces and immersive financial education tools.

Bitcoin's role in the metaverse goes far beyond being a simple currency. It represents a new paradigm for value creation, ownership, and commerce in virtual worlds. By providing a decentralized, secure, and interoperable financial system, Bitcoin enables users to navigate and succeed in the evolving digital economy.

As the metaverse expands, Bitcoin's integration will not only transform how we transact but also redefine our perceptions of ownership, creativity, and community in the virtual age. The rise of Bitcoin in the metaverse signals the dawn of a truly borderless, inclusive, and innovative economy.

Part 21. Altcoins vs. Bitcoin: The Eternal Debate

In the ever-evolving world of cryptocurrency, Bitcoin and altcoins represent two distinct but interconnected paths. Bitcoin, the original cryptocurrency, remains unmatched in its simplicity, reliability, and purpose. Altcoins, on the other hand, serve as a playground for innovation, continually pushing the boundaries of blockchain technology. However, their potential for high returns comes with more risks and volatility. This part dives deep into the dynamics of Bitcoin versus altcoins, exploring their unique roles, advantages, and challenges—and why I, Giannis Andreou, always keep at least 50% of my portfolio in Bitcoin.

1. Bitcoin: The Original, the Unique

A Singular Asset with No Equivalent

Bitcoin stands apart as the first cryptocurrency, and to this day, there is no second Bitcoin. It is unique not only because it was the first but because of what it has become—a symbol of financial sovereignty and decentralization.

Its purpose is clear and unchanging: to serve as a decentralized, censorship-resistant store of value and a medium of exchange. Unlike altcoins, Bitcoin doesn't attempt to cater to every niche or solve every problem. Its simplicity is its strength.

A Legacy of Resilience

Since its creation in 2009, Bitcoin has faced countless challenges: government bans, regulatory scrutiny, market crashes, and competition. Yet, it remains the most trusted and widely adopted cryptocurrency.

While technologies around it evolve, Bitcoin's core principles and network remain untouched, a testament to its resilience and universal appeal.

Why Bitcoin is Irreplaceable

Bitcoin represents more than a technological innovation—it's a global movement. It has become a hedge against inflation, a tool for financial freedom, and a foundational layer for the entire cryptocurrency ecosystem.

Unlike altcoins, Bitcoin's success doesn't depend on constant upgrades or trends. Its value lies in what it represents: trust, scarcity, and independence.

2. Altcoins: Innovation with Risks

Pioneering Technologies

Altcoins are where experimentation thrives. From smart contracts (Ethereum) to high-speed transactions (Solana) and interoperability (Polkadot), altcoins push blockchain technology into new territories.

Many altcoins address specific limitations of Bitcoin:

- Ethereum introduced programmability and became the backbone of decentralized finance (DeFi) and NFTs.

- Solana focuses on scalability, offering faster and cheaper transactions.

- Cardano emphasizes sustainability and rigorous research-based development.

Higher ROI, Higher Risk

Altcoins often offer incredible opportunities for high returns, especially during bull markets. Investors in projects like Ethereum or Solana early in their development have seen exponential growth.

However, the very innovation that makes altcoins attractive also makes them risky. Newer technologies can quickly disrupt existing altcoins, rendering them obsolete or significantly reducing their value.

Example: Early smart contract platforms like EOS or NEO have struggled to remain relevant as newer, more advanced projects like Avalanche or Polygon emerged.

Altcoins vs. Bitcoin in Stability

Unlike Bitcoin, which is rooted in a well-defined purpose, altcoins often depend on constant updates, community support, and market interest to thrive. That makes them more speculative and vulnerable to market cycles.

3. Bitcoin and Altcoins: Complementary Roles

Bitcoin as the Anchor

Bitcoin provides stability and a sense of security in a volatile market. It's the asset that many turn to during bear markets or times of economic uncertainty, as its reputation and history make it a trusted store of value.

For investors like myself, Bitcoin forms the foundation of a diversified portfolio. By holding at least 50% of my portfolio in Bitcoin, I ensure a strong base that balances the risks associated with altcoins.

Altcoins as the Growth Engine

Altcoins offer exposure to innovative sectors within the blockchain space. They cater to diverse use cases, from decentralized finance to gaming and supply chain management.

They complement Bitcoin's stability by adding growth potential to an investor's portfolio, but they require careful research and risk management.

4. Why Bitcoin Has No Equal

Not Just Technology, but Representation

Bitcoin's value lies not only in its technology but also in its symbolism. It represents decentralization, independence, and a hedge against traditional financial systems.

Unlike altcoins, Bitcoin's success isn't tied to continuous technological upgrades. It's a finished product—a digital asset designed to endure over time.

Resistant to Disruption

Altcoins often face disruption from newer projects that offer better scalability, speed, or features. Bitcoin, however, has remained undisrupted because of what it is and what it represents:

- Its decentralization ensures no single entity can control or alter it.
- Its widespread adoption and recognition give it unmatched network effects.

The Safety Net of Bitcoin

Bitcoin's simplicity and reliability make it a haven during market downturns. While altcoins may lose relevance, Bitcoin's role as a store of value ensures its longevity.

5. Lessons from an Investor's Perspective

Balancing Risk and Reward

For any investor, the key to navigating the cryptocurrency market is balance. Bitcoin offers stability, while altcoins provide growth. However, the speculative nature of altcoins means they should never outweigh the foundation Bitcoin offers.

My Portfolio Strategy

As someone who has experienced the highs and lows of the crypto market, I maintain at least 50% of my portfolio in Bitcoin. This approach allows me to:

- Capitalize on the growth of innovative altcoins without overexposing myself to their risks.
- Preserve long-term wealth in an asset I trust to endure economic and technological changes.

The Importance of Research

Investing in altcoins requires careful due diligence. Understanding the project's team, purpose, and competitive landscape is crucial, as not all altcoins survive or thrive.

6. Conclusion: Two Paths, One Ecosystem

Bitcoin and altcoins are not competitors; they are two sides of the same coin. Bitcoin offers stability, trust, and universality, making it the bedrock of the cryptocurrency world. Altcoins bring innovation and diversity, driving the ecosystem forward but with higher risks and rewards.

For me, and many others, Bitcoin remains irreplaceable. It is the foundation upon which all other investments are built. While altcoins offer exciting opportunities, there is no second Bitcoin. It stands out for its simplicity, resilience, and its role as the cornerstone of the cryptocurrency revolution.

Part 22. The Tax Side of Bitcoin

As Bitcoin transitions from a niche asset to a global phenomenon, governments worldwide have moved to regulate and tax its use. For investors and users alike, understanding the tax implications of Bitcoin is critical to maximizing returns and staying compliant with local laws. This part dives deep into practical strategies for managing Bitcoin-related taxes and highlights the diverse approaches to taxation across different countries.

1. Why Bitcoin Taxes Matter

A. Growing Regulatory Scrutiny

With Bitcoin's rise, tax authorities are paying closer attention to cryptocurrency transactions. Governments see crypto taxation as a means to generate revenue and ensure fair compliance within evolving financial systems.

Non-compliance can lead to fines, penalties, and legal challenges, making it essential for Bitcoin holders to stay informed.

B. Taxable Events in Bitcoin Transactions

Depending on your country, Bitcoin-related activities that could trigger a taxable event include:

1. Buying and Selling Bitcoin: Profits from selling Bitcoin are often subject to capital gains tax.
2. Using Bitcoin for Payments: Paying for goods or services with Bitcoin can trigger taxes based on the difference between the acquisition price and its market value at the time of the transaction.
3. Mining Bitcoin: Rewards earned from mining are typically treated as income and taxed accordingly.
4. Receiving Bitcoin as Income: Bitcoin received as payment for work or services is considered taxable income.

2. Practical Tips for Managing Bitcoin Taxes

A. Keep Detailed Records

Accurate record-keeping is the foundation of proper tax management.

Ensure you track the following:

- Dates and amounts of all Bitcoin transactions.

- The value of Bitcoin in your local currency at the time of each transaction.

- Associated fees (e.g., exchange or transfer fees).

Alternatively, you can use tools like Bitmerntaxes.com to automatically calculate your transactions and generate your tax report. As of the time of writing this book, Bitmerntaxes is available in Greece and Cyprus, with plans to expand to other countries in the future. You can check periodically or search for a similar tool available in your country.

B. Understand Your Tax Obligations

Research how your country classifies Bitcoin:
- Property or Asset: Many countries, including the U.S., treat Bitcoin as property, making capital gains taxes applicable.

- Currency: Some jurisdictions, like El Salvador, recognize Bitcoin as legal tender, simplifying tax requirements.

Understand the distinction between short-term and long-term gains:
- Short-term gains (assets held for less than a year) are typically taxed at higher rates.

- Long-term gains (assets held for over a year) usually enjoy lower tax rates.

C. Optimize Your Tax Strategy

- Tax-Loss Harvesting:
  Offset capital gains by selling Bitcoin at a loss, reducing your overall taxable income.
- Strategic Selling:
  Sell Bitcoin in a tax year where your overall income is lower to reduce tax liability.
- Donations:
  Donating Bitcoin to a recognized charity can provide tax benefits while supporting a cause you care about.

D. Consider Professional Guidance

Hiring a tax professional experienced in cryptocurrency can save you time and help you navigate complex regulations.
They can advise on:
- Filing requirements in your jurisdiction.
- Legal ways to minimize tax liabilities.
- Avoiding pitfalls like underreporting.

3. Global Differences in Crypto Tax Policies

A. Countries with High Taxation

1. United States:
   - Bitcoin is classified as property and is subject to capital gains tax. Taxpayers must report every transaction, including purchases and trades.
   - Mining rewards are taxed as regular income.
2. United Kingdom:
   - Bitcoin gains are subject to Capital Gains Tax (CGT) rules, with a personal allowance threshold before taxes are applied.
3. Australia:
   - Bitcoin is considered an asset for tax purposes, with gains taxed as capital gains. Regular traders are taxed on their profits as income.

B. Crypto Tax Havens
1. El Salvador:
   - The first country to adopt Bitcoin as legal tender. Bitcoin transactions are tax-free for foreign investors, attracting global interest.
2. Portugal:
   - No taxes on Bitcoin gains for individuals. However, businesses dealing in Bitcoin may face taxation.
3. United Arab Emirates (UAE):
   - No personal income tax or capital gains tax, making it a preferred destination for crypto investors.

C. Countries with Strict Regulations
1. India:
   - Bitcoin gains are taxed at a flat 30% rate, with no deductions allowed for losses.
   - A 1% Tax Deducted at Source (TDS) applies to all crypto transactions.
2. China:
   - Although crypto transactions are banned, mining activities and holdings may still face scrutiny in certain circumstances (until the moment of writing this book).

4. Common Challenges in Bitcoin Taxation

A. Complexity in Calculations

For active traders, calculating gains from multiple transactions and exchanges can be daunting.
Solution: Use automated tools to streamline the process.

B. Lack of Clear Regulations

Some countries still lack comprehensive crypto tax guidelines, leaving users unsure about their obligations.
Solution: Monitor updates from local tax authorities or consult experts.

C. Cross-Border Transactions

Using Bitcoin across borders can complicate tax reporting, especially when jurisdictions have conflicting rules.
Solution: Maintain detailed records and understand the tax implications in both countries.

5. The Future of Bitcoin Taxation

A. Increased Transparency

Governments are implementing stricter reporting requirements for crypto exchanges, such as the OECD's Crypto-Asset Reporting Framework (CARF).

Users should prepare for more stringent audits and reporting obligations.

B. Simplified Frameworks

Some jurisdictions are moving toward simplified taxation systems, such as flat rates or thresholds for crypto gains.

C. Potential for Global Standardization

International cooperation could lead to more consistent tax policies, reducing confusion for cross-border Bitcoin users.

6. My Approach as an Investor

As someone deeply involved in Bitcoin and cryptocurrency, I've learned that proper tax management is essential for long-term success. Here's my approach:

- I make sure that at least 50% of my portfolio is in Bitcoin, which simplifies tax calculations for long-term holdings.
- I regularly consult with tax professionals to optimize my strategy and ensure compliance with evolving regulations.

- Moving to crypto-friendly jurisdictions, like the UAE, has been a game-changer, enabling me to reinvest profits without heavy tax burdens.

The tax aspects of Bitcoin may seem complex, but with the right strategies and tools, they can be managed effectively. By staying informed about global tax policies and planning proactively, Bitcoin investors can minimize their liabilities while ensuring compliance. Whether you're a long-term holder, a trader, or a miner, understanding taxation is a crucial step in maximizing your Bitcoin journey.

Bitcoin offers financial freedom—but navigating its tax implications ensures you can enjoy that freedom without unnecessary risks.

Part 23. Real-World Adoption Trends: Nations Exploring Bitcoin

Bitcoin's journey from an experimental digital currency to a globally recognized asset has reached a pivotal stage as nations explore its potential as a legal tender, reserve asset, or tool for financial inclusion. While Bitcoin adoption by individuals and institutions has grown steadily, its use at the national level marks a new chapter in the cryptocurrency revolution.

This part explores real-world examples of countries adopting Bitcoin, with a focus on nations like Argentina, and Turkey, while examining the motivations, challenges, and implications of these decisions.

1. Argentina: Bitcoin as a Hedge Against Inflation

Argentina's long history of economic instability and hyperinflation has made Bitcoin an attractive alternative for citizens seeking to preserve their wealth.

A. The Inflation Crisis

With annual inflation rates surpassing 100% in 2023, the Argentine peso continues to lose purchasing power, depleting citizens' savings.

Bitcoin's scarcity and independence from government control make it a popular store of value in a country where trust in traditional financial institutions is limited.

B. Rising Adoption

- Bitcoin as Savings:
  As inflation rises, more Argentinians are using Bitcoin as a hedge, converting their pesos into BTC to preserve their wealth.

- Crypto Payroll:
  Freelancers and remote workers in Argentina often request payments in Bitcoin or stablecoins to avoid peso devaluation.

- Growing Merchant Use:
  Businesses in Argentina are adopting Bitcoin to attract customers and bypass banking restrictions.

C. Government Response

Despite Bitcoin's popularity, the Argentine government has implemented strict regulations to control capital flight and maintain monetary policy.

- High Taxes on Crypto Transactions:
  Bitcoin transactions are heavily taxed, and there are limits on crypto purchases made with pesos.

- Duality of Use:
  While Bitcoin adoption grows among citizens, the government remains cautious about its widespread use due to concerns about losing control over monetary policy.

2. Turkey: Bitcoin in a Currency Crisis

Turkey's economic challenges have also fueled significant Bitcoin adoption, particularly as the Turkish lira has experienced extreme devaluation.

A. The Lira's Collapse

Between 2018 and 2023, the Turkish lira lost more than 80% of its value, causing widespread economic instability.

Many Turks turned to Bitcoin as a hedge against the lira's collapse, viewing it as a more stable alternative.

B. Crypto Adoption Trends

- High Trading Volumes:

  Turkey ranks among the largest crypto markets in the world by trading volume, with citizens using Bitcoin both as a store of value and a medium of exchange.

- Integration into Daily Life:

  Businesses in Turkey are increasingly accepting Bitcoin for goods and services, particularly in urban centers like Istanbul.

C. Government Stance

The Turkish government initially imposed restrictions on cryptocurrency trading, citing concerns over fraud and money laundering.

However, growing public demand has prompted discussions about developing a regulatory framework that accommodates crypto while maintaining oversight.

3. Broader Trends in Nation-Level Adoption

A. Why Nations Explore Bitcoin

- Economic Resilience:

  Bitcoin's decentralization makes it less vulnerable to external shocks and local corruption.

- Geopolitical Strategy:

  Countries looking to reduce dependence on the U.S. dollar, such as Russia and Iran, have explored Bitcoin as an alternative for international trade.

B. Challenges for Governments

- Volatility:

  Bitcoin's price fluctuations make it a risky reserve asset for nations with limited resources.

- Regulatory Pushback:

  International organizations like the IMF have expressed concerns about Bitcoin adoption, warning that it could destabilize economies.

C. The Path Forward

- The experiences of countries like Argentina, and Turkey will shape future discussions on Bitcoin at the national level.

- Collaborative efforts between governments and the crypto industry could pave the way for smoother adoption and integration.

- The Trump Administration and the first 'Bitcoin President' is creating an optimization for worldwide adoption like never before.

The adoption of Bitcoin by nations in the real world serves as a testament to its transformative potential. Bitcoin is proving its value as more than just an investment.

However, adopting Bitcoin at the national level remains a complex challenge, requiring careful navigation of economic, political, and social factors. As more countries explore Bitcoin's possibilities, its role in the global financial system will continue to evolve, offering both opportunities and challenges in equal measure.

Part 24. Banks, Central Banks Adding Bitcoin to Their Reserves

Over the past decade, Bitcoin has evolved from a niche experiment to a globally recognized digital asset. One of the most significant signs of this evolution is its adoption by banks and central banks as part of their reserves. These entities, historically aligned with traditional financial systems, are now embracing Bitcoin for its potential as a store of value, inflation hedge, and portfolio diversifier.

This part explores the increasing trend of Bitcoin adoption by powerful entities and examines its implications for the global financial system.

1. Central Banks and Bitcoin: A Slow but Steady Shift

A. Central Banks Exploring Bitcoin

While no major central bank has officially added Bitcoin to its reserves, several are exploring its potential as part of their long-term strategies.

- El Salvador: As the first country to adopt Bitcoin as legal tender, its central bank now holds Bitcoin in its reserves to support national initiatives like Bitcoin-backed bonds.

- Smaller Economies: Countries with unstable currencies, such as Zimbabwe and Venezuela, have expressed interest in Bitcoin as a hedge against hyperinflation and reliance on foreign currencies.

B. Bitcoin as a Complement to Gold

Central banks traditionally hold gold as a safe-haven asset. Bitcoin is increasingly seen as 'digital gold,' providing similar benefits with enhanced portability and accessibility.

Potential Use Case: Bitcoin could act as a diversification tool for central banks, reducing reliance on the U.S. dollar in their reserves.

C. Challenges for Central Bank Adoption

- Volatility: Bitcoin's price fluctuations remain a concern for central banks seeking stability in their reserves.
- Regulatory Uncertainty: Many central banks are cautious about adopting Bitcoin due to the lack of global regulatory consensus.

2. Banks and Bitcoin: A Changing Dynamic

A. Banks Offering Bitcoin Services

Major banks, including JP Morgan Chase, Goldman Sachs, and Standard Chartered, have begun offering Bitcoin-related services such as:

- Custody solutions for institutional investors.
- Bitcoin trading desks for high-net-worth clients.
- Research and investment products tied to Bitcoin.

B. Bitcoin as a Hedge for Banks

Banks are increasingly adding Bitcoin to their reserves to hedge against macroeconomic risks, including inflation and devaluation of fiat currencies.

Example: Swiss private banks have been at the forefront, integrating Bitcoin into client portfolios as a hedge and growth asset.

C. The Role of Bitcoin ETFs

Bitcoin Exchange-Traded Funds (ETFs) offer banks and institutional clients exposure to Bitcoin without the need for direct custody.

The approval of Bitcoin spot ETFs in the U.S. and other regions has legitimized Bitcoin as an institutional asset.

3. The Advantages of Holding Bitcoin in Reserves

A. Inflation Hedge

Bitcoin's fixed supply of 21 million coins makes it an attractive hedge against inflation, particularly as central banks continue quantitative easing and fiat currencies lose purchasing power.

B. Portfolio Diversification

Adding Bitcoin to reserves reduces overall risk by diversifying asset classes.

Studies have shown that even a small allocation (1-5%) of Bitcoin in a portfolio can improve risk-adjusted returns.

C. Increasing Demand

Institutional adoption creates a feedback loop: as more banks and central banks add Bitcoin to their reserves, its demand and legitimacy grow, further solidifying its value proposition.

4. Implications for the Global Financial System

A. Shifting Power Dynamics

The inclusion of Bitcoin in reserves by central banks and institutions could reduce reliance on traditional reserve currencies like the U.S. dollar, potentially reshaping global financial power structures.

B. Accelerating Adoption

The participation of respected institutions in the Bitcoin ecosystem legitimizes it in the eyes of skeptics, paving the way for broader adoption by individuals, corporations, and governments.

C. Potential Risks

- Over-reliance on the performance of Bitcoin could expose institutions to market volatility.
- Regulatory developments could either enhance or hinder the adoption trajectory.

5. My Perspective as an Investor

- Having spent over a decade in the cryptocurrency space, I see this trend as a strong validation of Bitcoin's long-term potential.
- Institutions and banks recognizing Bitcoin as a reserve asset highlight its transition from speculative investment to a foundational part of the financial system.
- I allocate 50% of my portfolio to Bitcoin, not just as a store of value but as a reflection of its transformative power.

Bitcoin's role in reserves is no longer a question of 'if' but 'when' and 'how extensively.' As adoption grows, the line between traditional finance and the decentralized economy will continue to blur, paving the way for a more resilient and inclusive financial future.

Part 25. Scenarios for Bitcoin as a Global Reserve Currency

Bitcoin's potential to evolve from a niche digital asset into a global reserve currency is no longer a far-fetched idea. As the world grapples with economic uncertainty, inflation, and shifts in financial power, Bitcoin's unique characteristics—decentralization, scarcity, and resilience—position it as a credible contender for global reserve status. However, this transition would require significant shifts in global economic structures and widespread adoption by governments, institutions, and central banks. This part explores the scenarios under which Bitcoin could become a global reserve currency and provides insights from economists, Bitcoin advocates, and critics.

Scenario 1: U.S. Dollar Weakening Due to Inflation or Debt Crises

A. Rising Concerns About the U.S. Dollar

The U.S. dollar has served as the primary reserve currency of the world since the mid-20th century, but its dominance is increasingly being questioned due to:

- Quantitative Easing (QE): Excessive money printing has led to concerns about long-term inflation and devaluation of the dollar.
- Rising National Debt: The U.S. debt surpassed $36 trillion in 2024, raising doubts about its sustainability and global trust in the dollar.

B. Bitcoin as a Hedge Against Dollar Devaluation

With its finite supply of 21 million coins, Bitcoin presents an attractive alternative to fiat currencies, which can be devalued through inflationary policies.

As confidence in the dollar weakens, countries may seek to diversify their reserves with assets like Bitcoin to reduce dependency on U.S. monetary policy.

C. Historical Parallels

The transition from gold-backed currencies to fiat in the 20th century illustrates how economic shifts can lead to new reserve standards. Bitcoin could follow a similar trajectory, replacing fiat currencies as a global standard for value.

Scenario 2: Broader Adoption by Institutional Investors and Governments

A. Institutional Adoption Drives Legitimacy

The increasing adoption of Bitcoin by institutions such as BlackRock, Fidelity, and MicroStrategy lends credibility to its role as a store of value.

- Institutional Bitcoin ETFs and funds have made it easier for governments and banks to hold Bitcoin indirectly.

- As institutions allocate higher portions of their portfolios to Bitcoin, it reinforces its position as a trusted asset.

B. Sovereign Wealth Funds and Bitcoin

- Governments managing sovereign wealth funds, such as Norway's Government Pension Fund, are exploring Bitcoin as part of their diversification strategies.

- Countries seeking to hedge against geopolitical risks may allocate a portion of their reserves to Bitcoin to reduce reliance on traditional assets like U.S. Treasury bonds.

Scenario 3: Integration into Central Bank Digital Currencies (CBDCs)

A. The Rise of CBDCs

Central banks worldwide are developing digital currencies to modernize payment systems and improve financial inclusivity.

Examples include China's digital yuan, the European Central Bank's digital euro, and the Federal Reserve's exploration of a digital dollar.

B. Bitcoin's Role in a CBDC Ecosystem

While CBDCs are centralized, Bitcoin could complement these systems as a reserve asset underpinning their value.

For countries with weak fiat currencies, using Bitcoin as collateral for their CBDC could enhance trust and stability.

Bitcoin-backed CBDCs would combine the benefits of digital currency with the scarcity and security of Bitcoin.

C. Challenges and Opportunities

Central banks may resist Bitcoin integration due to concerns about losing control over monetary policy.

However, countries facing hyperinflation or struggling with currency instability may adopt Bitcoin as a stabilizing mechanism in their digital currency frameworks.

Predictions and Opinions

A. Bitcoin Advocates

- Michael Saylor (MicroStrategy CEO): "Bitcoin is digital gold, and it will eventually replace gold as the primary reserve asset of the 21st century."

- Cathie Wood (ARK Invest CEO): Predicts Bitcoin could reach $1.5 million per coin by 2030, driven by institutional and sovereign adoption.

- Max Keiser (American TV producer): Argues that Bitcoin is the ultimate tool for financial sovereignty and will become the world's dominant currency as trust in fiat systems erodes.

B. Economists and Neutral Observers

Some economists see Bitcoin as a viable hedge against inflation but remain skeptical about its role as a reserve currency due to its price volatility.

- Nouriel Roubini: Criticizes Bitcoin as too unstable to serve as a reserve currency, though he acknowledges its growing adoption as a speculative asset.

- Ray Dalio: Suggests Bitcoin could complement gold as an asset in reserve portfolios.

C. Critics' Concerns

- Bitcoin's volatility remains a significant hurdle to function as a stable reserve currency.

- Critics argue that widespread government adoption may take decades due to regulatory resistance and the need for technological integration.

Factors Influencing Bitcoin's Transition

A. Global Economic Shifts

Major geopolitical or economic crises could accelerate the transition to alternative reserve assets like Bitcoin.

Example: A significant devaluation of the dollar or euro could push nations toward Bitcoin.

B. Technological Advancements

Scaling solutions like the Lightning Network could make Bitcoin more practical for global financial systems, addressing concerns about transaction speed and cost.

C. Regulatory Evolution

Clear regulations and frameworks for Bitcoin adoption by governments and institutions will be crucial for its transition into a worldwide reserve asset.

Bitcoin's path to becoming a global reserve currency is not guaranteed but remains a real possibility. Scenarios such as the weakening of the U.S. dollar, broader institutional and government adoption, and integration into CBDCs highlight how Bitcoin could achieve this status.

While challenges like volatility and regulatory resistance persist, Bitcoin's unique characteristics—its scarcity, decentralization, and trustless nature—position it as a compelling alternative to traditional reserve assets. Whether Bitcoin fully transitions into a global reserve currency or remains a powerful store of value, its influence on the worldwide financial system is undeniable and continues to grow each year.

Part 26. What It Means for Individuals: Preparing for a Bitcoin-Driven World

As Bitcoin approaches mainstream adoption and the potential to become a global reserve currency, individuals can benefit significantly—but only if they are prepared. Whether for savings, investments, or participation in international trade, Bitcoin's potential transformation of the financial landscape will bring both opportunities and challenges.

This part explores how individuals can position themselves for a Bitcoin-driven world and the implications for personal finance and global trade dynamics.

1. Preparing for a Bitcoin Reserve Currency Era

A. Financial Education

Understanding Bitcoin:
- Learn the fundamentals of Bitcoin—how it works, why it's scarce, and how to secure it safely, either with hardware wallets or other security methods.
- Stay informed about Bitcoin's role in global economics to better anticipate shifts in its adoption and value.

Monitoring Policy Changes:
- Stay updated on governmental and institutional decisions regarding Bitcoin adoption, regulation, and integration into financial systems.

B. Acquiring Bitcoin Strategically

Dollar-Cost Averaging (DCA):
- Gradually accumulate Bitcoin over time to mitigate the impact of price volatility.

Portfolio Allocation:
- Allocate a portion of your investments to Bitcoin based on your risk tolerance. As Bitcoin becomes more prominent, many financial advisors recommend 5-10% of a portfolio for moderate-risk investors, while higher allocations may appeal to those with greater risk appetite.

Long-Term Holding:
- Treat Bitcoin as a long-term asset rather than a short-term speculative tool, aligning your investment strategy with its potential future as a reserve currency.

C. Developing Technical Literacy

Wallet Management:
- Learn how to use hardware wallets and multi-signature setups to secure your Bitcoin.

Transaction Skills:
- Familiarize yourself with sending, receiving, and managing Bitcoin transactions, especially using Layer 2 solutions like the Lightning Network for faster and cheaper payments.

D. Investments: Diversification and Growth

Increased Demand:
- As Bitcoin adoption grows, its value is expected to rise, benefiting long-term investors.

New Financial Products:
- The development of Bitcoin ETFs, lending platforms, and derivatives provides new ways for individuals to grow their wealth through Bitcoin.

Challenges to Consider:
- Bitcoin's price volatility may still affect short-term investments, requiring careful planning and risk management.

E. Generational Wealth

Planning for Inheritance:
- Bitcoin's digital nature requires clear strategies for passing it on to heirs, such as creating a well-documented seed phrase backup and educating family members about its use.

Multi-Generational Wealth:
- Bitcoin's potential as a global reserve currency makes it a powerful tool for building long-term wealth that can be inherited across generations.

2. Impact on Global Trade Dynamics

A. Borderless Commerce

Universal Currency:
- Bitcoin's borderless nature eliminates the need for currency conversions, reducing costs and barriers in international trade.
- Individuals participating in global commerce, such as freelancers or small businesses, can transact seamlessly with Bitcoin.

Decentralized Payments:
- Bitcoin allows peer-to-peer transactions, bypassing banks and reducing reliance on intermediaries.

B. Enhanced Financial Sovereignty

Independent Wealth Control:
- Individuals can participate in global trade without restrictions from capital controls or currency devaluation imposed by governments.

Economic Participation:
- People in underbanked regions can use Bitcoin to access global markets, leveling the playing field for economic participation.

C. Trade Efficiencies

Lower Transaction Costs:

- Traditional trade payments often involve fees for wire transfers or currency exchanges. Bitcoin reduces these costs, making global trade more efficient.

Faster Settlements:

- Bitcoin's near-instant settlement capability via solutions like the Lightning Network accelerates payment timelines, enhancing trade efficiency.

3. Challenges Individuals May Face

A. Volatility

Bitcoin's price fluctuations can make it challenging to predict its value in the short term, requiring careful financial planning for those relying on it for savings or trade.

B. Security Risks

Managing private keys and wallets requires vigilance to avoid loss or theft.

Lack of education and technical literacy may deter some individuals from adopting Bitcoin as a primary financial tool.

4. Practical Steps for Individuals

1. Start Small:
   Begin by acquiring a small amount of Bitcoin and learning the basics of wallet management and security.

2. Stay Informed:
   Follow trusted sources for updates on Bitcoin adoption, regulation, and technological advancements.

3. Integrate Gradually:
   Use Bitcoin alongside traditional financial tools to ensure a smooth transition as its adoption grows.

The rise of Bitcoin as a global reserve currency has profound implications for individuals. By preparing now—through education, strategic investment, and integration into everyday transactions—individuals can thrive in a Bitcoin-driven world.

Bitcoin offers unparalleled opportunities for financial sovereignty, wealth preservation, and participation in global trade. For those willing to embrace its potential, the journey toward a decentralized and inclusive economic future is one of empowerment and unprecedented opportunity.

Part 27. A Vision of the Future

Imagine a world where Bitcoin achieves mass adoption, where financial systems are freed from the constraints of borders, central banks, and the limitations of fiat currencies. In this vision, Bitcoin is not just a digital currency—it's the foundation of a new global economic paradigm. Its impact reshapes society, politics, and finance, creating opportunities and challenges that redefine how humanity interacts with money, power, and each other.

1. A Financially Sovereign Society

Empowered Individuals

In a Bitcoin-driven future, individuals gain full control over their finances. There's no longer a need to rely on banks or intermediaries to access, store, or transfer wealth.

With Bitcoin as a universal medium of exchange, people in underbanked regions finally participate in the global economy, bridging the gap between the privileged and the underserved.

Financial Inclusion

Farmers in rural Africa, entrepreneurs in South America, or workers in Asia can transact with the same ease as anyone in developed nations. Bitcoin becomes a tool for equality, enabling a truly global economy.

2. Transforming Politics and Power Structures

Decentralized Financial Power

Central banks and governments lose their monopoly on money creation. The ability to manipulate currencies through inflationary policies becomes a relic of the past.

Political corruption tied to financial control diminishes as Bitcoin's blockchain ensures transparency and accountability in financial dealings.

Resilient Economies

Nations embracing Bitcoin develop resilient economies not particularly dependent on the dollar or other reserve currencies. This shift reduces geopolitical tensions tied to monetary policy and currency hegemony.

Example: Countries previously reliant on foreign aid or unstable fiat currencies can stabilize their economies through Bitcoin adoption.

3. Redefining Global Finance

Seamless Global Trade

With Bitcoin as a universal currency, cross-border trade becomes frictionless. Businesses no longer face currency exchange risks, high transaction fees, or delays caused by traditional financial systems.

Microtransactions flourish, enabling entirely new industries and economic models that were previously unfeasible.

A New Store of Value

Bitcoin replaces gold and fiat currencies as the primary reserve asset. Its scarcity and predictability make it the anchor of the global financial system.

Central banks transition from printing money to managing digital reserves, fundamentally altering their role in the economy.

Decentralized Finance at Scale

As decentralized finance (DeFi) evolves, it is powered by Bitcoin's security and simplicity. Individuals earn, lend, and invest directly through decentralized platforms, bypassing traditional financial institutions.

4. Social and Cultural Impacts

A Generation of Financial Literacy

As Bitcoin becomes mainstream, financial literacy becomes a global priority. People understand the value of saving, investing, and securing their wealth, leading to a more informed and empowered society.

Cultural Shift Toward Sovereignty

The philosophy behind Bitcoin—freedom, privacy, and decentralization—is ingrained in global culture. Society moves away from dependence on centralized systems, fostering innovation and self-reliance.

Economic Equality

While Bitcoin alone cannot resolve systemic inequalities, its neutrality and accessibility offer individuals the tools to escape financial oppression and build wealth independently.

5. Challenges on the Road to Adoption

Resistance from Power Structures

Governments and institutions benefiting from the current system may resist Bitcoin's rise, creating regulatory hurdles and potential conflicts.

Traditional financial institutions must evolve or risk obsolescence in the face of decentralized alternatives.

Adapting to a New System

Societies must navigate the challenges of transitioning to a Bitcoin-based economy, including technological education, infrastructure development, and addressing concerns like energy usage.

6. The Journey Ahead

Incremental Adoption

Bitcoin's path to mass adoption is unlikely to be abrupt. It will evolve through phases: increasing institutional use, growing national adoption, and finally, becoming a universal standard.

Each step will bring new use cases, innovations, and challenges, reinforcing Bitcoin's place in the global financial system.

A Coexistence of Systems

Even in a world dominated by Bitcoin, fiat currencies may coexist in specific contexts. Bitcoin's role would complement, not entirely replace, existing systems for decades to come.

Bitcoin's Promise

Bitcoin's rise is more than a financial revolution—it's a rethinking of how humanity interacts with value, power, and opportunity. It offers a future where wealth is accessible, control is decentralized, and trust is placed in code rather than fallible institutions.

This vision is ambitious and will require perseverance, innovation, and adaptation. However, the foundation has already been laid. Bitcoin has proven its resilience and utility, inspiring millions to rethink their relationship with money. As we stand on the cusp of this transformation, one thing is clear: Bitcoin is not just a currency; it's a movement that could redefine the future of global finance and society.

GLOSSARY

21 Million Cap
The maximum number of Bitcoins that will ever exist. This built-in scarcity is one of the reasons Bitcoin is valuable.

Altcoins
Any cryptocurrency other than Bitcoin. Examples include Ethereum and Solana.

ASIC miner
An application-specific integrated circuit (ASIC) miner is a computerized device that uses ASICs for the sole purpose of mining bitcoin or another mineable cryptocurrency.

Bear Market
It refers to a period in which the prices of cryptocurrencies or other financial assets decline continuously and significantly, usually due to negative market conditions or investor concerns. It is characterized by a lack of confidence and a downward trend.

Bitcoin Adoption Curve
The rate at which Bitcoin is being adopted worldwide, similar to how smartphones or the internet spread.

Bitcoin City
A city in El Salvador powered by Bitcoin, built to attract innovation and investment.

Bitcoin Core
The main software used to interact with Bitcoin. It's maintained by developers worldwide.

Bitcoin ETFs
Investment funds that track Bitcoin's price, letting people invest without owning Bitcoin directly.

Bitcoin Maximalist
Someone who believes Bitcoin is superior to all other cryptocurrencies.

Bitcoin Mining Pools
Groups of miners who combine their computing power to increase the chances of earning Bitcoin rewards.

Bitcoiners
People who support or invest in Bitcoin.

Blockchain
It is a decentralized digital chain of data blocks, which records transactions in a secure, transparent and immutable manner, operating without the need for a central authority and is shared across many computing devices worldwide.

Blockchain Forks
Splits in the blockchain that create new cryptocurrencies. They happen when developers disagree on Bitcoin's future.

BTC
Bitcoin (BTC) is a cryptocurrency (a virtual currency) designed to act as money and a form of payment outside the control of any one person, group, or entity.

Capital Gains Tax
A tax you pay on profits when selling Bitcoin or other assets.

CBDC
A central bank digital currency (CBDC - also called digital fiat currency or digital base money) is a digital currency issued by a central bank, rather than by a commercial bank. It is also a liability of the central bank and denominated in the sovereign currency, as is the case with physical banknotes and coins.

Censorship-Resistant
Bitcoin transactions can't be blocked or controlled by governments or banks.

Cold Storage
Storing Bitcoin offline, away from hackers, often using hardware wallets.

Custody Services
Companies that securely hold Bitcoin for you, like a digital vault.

Cypherpunk
A movement that advocates for privacy, freedom, and decentralization using technology like Bitcoin.

Decentralization
A system where no single person, company, or government controls the network. Bitcoin operates through a global network of computers instead of a central authority.

Decentralized Autonomous Organizations (DAOs)
Organizations run by code instead of people, allowing decentralized decision-making.

DeFi (Decentralized Finance)
Financial tools built on blockchain, allowing you to borrow, lend, or invest without a bank.

Digital Asset
Anything valuable that exists digitally, like Bitcoin or NFTs.

Digital Gold
A term used to describe Bitcoin's role as a modern, digital version of gold for storing wealth.

Dollar-Cost Averaging (DCA)
With a dollar-cost averaging strategy, you invest a set amount at regular intervals, no matter how stock prices change. The goal of dollar-cost averaging is to lessen the effects of price fluctuations and lower your average per-share cost over time.

ETFs (Exchange-Traded Funds)
It is a mutual fund that is traded on a stock exchange.

Fiat Currency
Traditional government-issued money like the U.S. dollar or euro. It has value because governments declare it does.

Forks
When developers create a new version of Bitcoin by splitting the blockchain. Examples include Bitcoin Cash, created to improve transaction speed.

GDP (Gross Domestic Product)
The total value of all goods and services produced within a country over a specific period. It's used to measure its economic performance.

Gen Z
Generation Z (often shortened to Gen Z), also known as Zoomers, is the demographic cohort succeeding Millennials. Researchers and popular media use the mid-to-late 1990s as starting birth years and the early 2010s as ending birth years, with the generation most frequently being defined as people born from 1997 to 2012.

Genesis Block
The first block ever created in the Bitcoin blockchain. It marked the start of Bitcoin in 2009.

Global South
The nations of the world which are regarded as having a relatively low level of economic and industrial development, and are typically located to the south of more industrialized nations.

Halving
An event every four years when Bitcoin rewards for miners are cut in half, making Bitcoin even scarcer.

Hash - Hashing
Hashing in blockchain is a cryptographic process where data, like transaction details in a block, is converted into a fixed-length string of characters, known as a hash. Hash is this unique digital fingerprint ensures data integrity and immutability.

HODL
A playful term meaning 'Hold On for Dear Life.' It encourages Bitcoin investors to hold their coins long-term.

HODLers
Bitcoin investors who hold onto their coins through price swings, believing in Bitcoin's long-term value.

Hyperinflation
When prices rise so fast that a country's currency becomes almost worthless. Think Venezuela or Zimbabwe.

Immutable Ledger
The blockchain's records can't be changed, making Bitcoin transactions permanent and secure.

Inflation Hedge
Investments like Bitcoin that help protect your money's value when prices rise.

Layer 2 Solution
Add-on technologies, like the Lightning Network, that improve Bitcoin's speed and usability without changing the main blockchain.

Legal Tender
Money that must be accepted for payments within a country, like Bitcoin in El Salvador.

Lightning Network
A system built on top of Bitcoin that makes transactions faster and cheaper by processing them off the main blockchain.

Memecoin
Cryptocurrencies created as jokes, often highly speculative.

Metaverse
A virtual, interconnected 3D universe where people can interact, socialize, work, and play using avatars, often combining augmented reality (AR), virtual reality (VR), and blockchain technologies.

MiCA (Markets in Crypto-Assets Regulation)
An EU regulation that sets rules for cryptocurrencies to protect consumers and businesses.

Millennials
Also known as Generation Y or Gen Y, is the demographic cohort preceding Generation Z. Researchers and popular media use the early 1980s as starting birth years and the mid-1990s to early 2000s as ending birth years, with the generation typically being defined as people born from 1981 to 1996.

Mining
The process of using powerful computers to solve puzzles. Miners validate transactions and add them to the blockchain, earning Bitcoin as a reward.

Multi-Signature Wallets (Multisig)
Wallets that need multiple approvals (like two or three passwords) to access funds, adding extra security.

NFT (Non-Fungible Token)
A unique digital asset representing ownership of a specific item or piece of content, such as art, music, or videos, verified on a blockchain.

Nodes
Computers that store and share a copy of the entire Bitcoin blockchain, ensuring the network runs smoothly.

Nonce
Short for "number used once," a nonce is a unique number central to the mining process, essential for adding new blocks to a blockchain. A nonce is a random or semi-random number that miners adjust to solve complex cryptographic puzzles.

P2P (Peer-to-Peer)
Peer-to-peer (P2P) lending makes it possible for individuals to obtain loans directly from other individuals, without going through a bank or other financial institution. The platforms that provide this type of

lending are called P2P Platforms.

Payment Channels
Private paths on the Lightning Network that process Bitcoin transactions instantly and cheaply.

Proof of Stake (PoS)
It is a blockchain consensus mechanism where participants are selected to validate transactions and create new blocks based on the amount of cryptocurrencies they hold and 'lock' (staking). It is more energy efficient than Proof of Work.

Proof of Work (PoW)
A security system that requires miners to solve complex problems to confirm transactions. It makes Bitcoin safe from fraud and manipulation.

Property Classification
Bitcoin is classified as property in some countries, meaning it's treated like real estate or stocks.

Quantum Computing
A type of computing that uses quantum bits (qubits) to perform complex calculations much faster than traditional computers. Quantum Bits are the basic units of information in quantum computing, capable of representing 0, 1, or both simultaneously (superposition).

Quantum Computing Threat
A potential future issue where advanced computers could crack Bitcoin's encryption. Developers are already preparing for this.

Reserve Currency
A currency, like the U.S. dollar, that countries hold in reserves to stabilize their economies. Bitcoin might become one someday.

Satoshi Nakamoto
The mysterious creator(s) of Bitcoin. No one knows who they are or where they live.

Satoshis (Sats)
The smallest unit of Bitcoin, like cents to a dollar. One Bitcoin equals 100 million satoshis.

SegWit (Segregated Witness)
A past upgrade that made Bitcoin transactions faster and reduced fees by changing how transaction data is stored.

SHA-256 algorithm
SHA means Secure Hashing Algorithm. SHA-256 is an algorithm in the family of cryptographic hash functions. The '256' in its name refers to the length of the hash that it produces, which is 256 bits. This algorithm plays a critical role in ensuring data integrity and security in digital communications.

Sidechains
Separate blockchains connected to Bitcoin for testing new features or supporting additional services.

Smart Contracts
Digital agreements that are automatically executed when conditions are met.

Stablecoins
Stablecoins are cryptocurrencies designed to maintain a fixed value, usually pegged to a traditional currency, such as the dollar or euro. This stability is achieved through the use of collateral or algorithms that balance the supply of the token. Stablecoins are primarily used for transactions, stores of value, and as a means of hedging risk in the cryptocurrency world.

Staking
It is the process by which users hold and 'lock' their cryptocurrencies in a network to support its operation, such as confirming transactions or creating new blocks. They are rewarded with additional coins in return for securing and maintaining the network. It is a form of investment that provides passive income to participants.

Store of Value
An asset, like gold or Bitcoin, that keeps its value over time and protects against inflation.

SWIFT
SWIFT (Society for Worldwide Interbank Financial Telecommunications) is a global member-owned cooperative that functions as a huge messaging system. Members (banks and other financial institutions) use it to quickly, accurately, and securely send and receive information, primarily money transfer instructions.

Taproot Upgrade
A technical update that improved Bitcoin's privacy and allowed for more complex transactions, like smart contracts.

Whitepaper (in crypto)
A cryptocurrency white paper is a document that summarizes the important information on a blockchain or cryptocurrency project. It normally includes a project's goals, products, features, the parameters that give the cryptocurrency its economic value, and information about the project's participants.

REFERENCES

This book contains information and data, as well as definitions of terms taken from the following sources:

Wikipedia.org

Theblockbeats.info

Bitcoin Magazine

Information, data, terms, and definitions have also been taken from the respective platforms, exchanges, or applications mentioned in the book.

ABOUT THE AUTHOR

Giannis Andreou is a dynamic entrepreneur and self-made businessman with over 15 years of experience leading innovative ventures. As the visionary founder of **Bitmern Group**, a trailblazing conglomerate that includes companies such as Bitmern Capital, Bitmern Taxes, Bitmern Staking, and Bitmern Agency, Giannis has revolutionized the blockchain and cryptocurrency landscape.

Guided by mentorship from top billionaires, he has emerged as a prominent thought leader and social media influencer, creating over **4,000 video pieces** in just four years. His platform is recognized as the **#1 cryptocurrency channel in Greece and Cyprus**, reaching a global audience with valuable insights and strategies.

Giannis is also a prolific author of three books and the creator of six online courses, empowering individuals to excel in topics such as blockchain, personal finance, and wealth creation. **Now, by expanding his knowledge and experience worldwide through his online education content**, he aims to inspire and equip a global audience to embrace innovation and financial empowerment.

His expertise spans **blockchain and cryptocurrencies, online and offline marketing, sales, e-commerce, social media branding, public speaking,** and **affiliate marketing**.

With an unwavering passion for innovation and education, Giannis Andreou continues to inspire readers and audiences to achieve financial freedom and embrace the transformative power of blockchain technology.

Follow Giannis Andreou on social media by scanning the QR code on the next page.

Follow Giannis Andreou on social media.

Scan Below

www.ingramcontent.com/pod-product-compliance
Lightning Source LLC
LaVergne TN
LVHW051438050326
832903LV00030BD/3153